IRAN'S NONCOMPLIANCE WITH ITS INTERNATIONAL ATOMIC ENERGY AGENCY OBLIGATIONS

HEARING

BEFORE THE

SUBCOMMITTEE ON
THE MIDDLE EAST AND NORTH AFRICA

OF THE

COMMITTEE ON FOREIGN AFFAIRS
HOUSE OF REPRESENTATIVES

ONE HUNDRED FOURTEENTH CONGRESS

FIRST SESSION

MARCH 24, 2015

Serial No. 114–23

Printed for the use of the Committee on Foreign Affairs

Available via the World Wide Web: http://www.foreignaffairs.house.gov/ or
http://www.gpo.gov/fdsys/

U.S. GOVERNMENT PUBLISHING OFFICE

93–913PDF   WASHINGTON : 2015

COMMITTEE ON FOREIGN AFFAIRS

EDWARD R. ROYCE, California, *Chairman*

CHRISTOPHER H. SMITH, New Jersey
ILEANA ROS-LEHTINEN, Florida
DANA ROHRABACHER, California
STEVE CHABOT, Ohio
JOE WILSON, South Carolina
MICHAEL T. McCAUL, Texas
TED POE, Texas
MATT SALMON, Arizona
DARRELL E. ISSA, California
TOM MARINO, Pennsylvania
JEFF DUNCAN, South Carolina
MO BROOKS, Alabama
PAUL COOK, California
RANDY K. WEBER SR., Texas
SCOTT PERRY, Pennsylvania
RON DeSANTIS, Florida
MARK MEADOWS, North Carolina
TED S. YOHO, Florida
CURT CLAWSON, Florida
SCOTT DesJARLAIS, Tennessee
REID J. RIBBLE, Wisconsin
DAVID A. TROTT, Michigan
LEE M. ZELDIN, New York
TOM EMMER, Minnesota

ELIOT L. ENGEL, New York
BRAD SHERMAN, California
GREGORY W. MEEKS, New York
ALBIO SIRES, New Jersey
GERALD E. CONNOLLY, Virginia
THEODORE E. DEUTCH, Florida
BRIAN HIGGINS, New York
KAREN BASS, California
WILLIAM KEATING, Massachusetts
DAVID CICILLINE, Rhode Island
ALAN GRAYSON, Florida
AMI BERA, California
ALAN S. LOWENTHAL, California
GRACE MENG, New York
LOIS FRANKEL, Florida
TULSI GABBARD, Hawaii
JOAQUIN CASTRO, Texas
ROBIN L. KELLY, Illinois
BRENDAN F. BOYLE, Pennsylvania

AMY PORTER, *Chief of Staff*   THOMAS SHEEHY, *Staff Director*
JASON STEINBAUM, *Democratic Staff Director*

SUBCOMMITTEE ON THE MIDDLE EAST AND NORTH AFRICA

ILEANA ROS-LEHTINEN, Florida, *Chairman*

STEVE CHABOT, Ohio
JOE WILSON, South Carolina
DARRELL E. ISSA, California
RANDY K. WEBER SR., Texas
RON DeSANTIS, Florida
MARK MEADOWS, North Carolina
TED S. YOHO, Florida
CURT CLAWSON, Florida
DAVID A. TROTT, Michigan
LEE M. ZELDIN, New York

THEODORE E. DEUTCH, Florida
GERALD E. CONNOLLY, Virginia
BRIAN HIGGINS, New York
DAVID CICILLINE, Rhode Island
ALAN GRAYSON, Florida
GRACE MENG, New York
LOIS FRANKEL, Florida
BRENDAN F. BOYLE, Pennsylvania

CONTENTS

_____

IRAN'S NONCOMPLIANCE WITH ITS INTERNATIONAL ATOMIC ENERGY AGENCY OBLIGATIONS

TUESDAY, MARCH 24, 2015

HOUSE OF REPRESENTATIVES,
SUBCOMMITTEE ON THE MIDDLE EAST AND NORTH AFRICA,
COMMITTEE ON FOREIGN AFFAIRS,
Washington, DC.

The committee met, pursuant to notice, at 2 o'clock p.m., in room 2172 Rayburn House Office Building, Hon. Ileana Ros-Lehtinen (chairman of the subcommittee) presiding.

Ms. ROS-LEHTINEN. The subcommittee will come to order. After recognizing myself and Ranking Member Ted Deutch for 5 minutes each for our opening statements, I will be glad to recognize other members seeking recognition for 1 minute. We will then hear from our witnesses. Thank you, ladies and gentlemen, for being here today. Without objection, the witnesses' prepared statements will be made a part of the record and members may have 5 days to insert statements and questions for the record, subject to the length limitation in the rules.

Before we begin, I would like to see unanimous consent to enter the testimony of AEI's Dr. Mike Rubin for the record. Dr. Rubin was originally slated to testify at this hearing before it had to be postponed due to inclement weather earlier this month and is not unable to join us today and we thank him for his contributions to this hearing. And hearing no objections, his statement will be made a part of the record.

The chair now recognizes herself for 5 minutes. This week marks the end of the second extension of the Joint Plan of Action and though no final deal has been made as the negotiations continue, it is important to take stock of where we stand today versus where we stood on November 24, 2013 when the JPOA was formally announced. While Iran may have complied with some cosmetic aspects of the JPOA, reducing enrichment stockpiles, turning off some centrifuges, the fact remains that Iran's nuclear infrastructure remains entirely intact.

Let us pretend for a moment that Iran hasn't already violated the terms of the JPOA, a notion that is as preposterous as Iran's claim to its right of enrichment. The role of monitoring Iran's nuclear program and verifying its adherence to the agreement falls on the International Atomic Energy Agency, the IAEA, and our Intelligence Community. Neither option inspires much confidence considering we failed to detect Iran's covert activity before and we failed to detect nuclear activity in Syria and North Korea in the past.

History has shown us that our intelligence assessments are not always perfect, so we cannot allow Iran to even possess the capability to get a bomb because we very likely would miss it if Iran makes that mad dash.

Just last year, the Defense Department put out its own assessment that we do, in fact, lack the capability to detect covert nuclear sites in Iran and wouldn't be able to detect a move toward breakout. And it was before this subcommittee that General Hayden, former Director of the NSA and the CIA, echoed that sentiment saying that as long as Iran continues to block access to its facilities we wouldn't be able to detect its development of a bomb. He then stated that if he were advising the President, unless Iran came clean about its past weaponization and PMD activities, he would be compelled to say that the deal could not be adequately verified. So then that leaves the lion's share to the IAEA.

The IAEA has a long history in Iran, but not nearly as long as Iran's history of subterfuge and covert work on a nuclear weapons program. As a signatory to the NPT and the Safeguard Agreement with the IAEA since 1974, Iran was required to make accurate and complete declarations of all of its nuclear material and nuclear-related activities to the IAEA. We know that Iran was in violation of this for decades and being in violation had forfeited any claim it had to enriching uranium.

Since 2003, we know that Iran has done everything it can to deceive, block, and prevent the IAEA from gaining the access it needs to verify its nuclear program. Iran has taken advantage of several rounds of negotiations to stall for time and has exploited loopholes and ambiguities to make advances in its nuclear program. And this latest attempt by the P5+1 is no different. Since November 24, 2013, as part of the JPOA, the IAEA has been working to get unresolved issues regarding Iran's past, its work on nuclear weapons development, and other possible military dimensions (PMD) of Tehran's nuclear program.

Yet, even as the negotiations continue, the IAEA reports that Iran has been unwilling to cooperate and is hindering its inquiries. There are still a dozen outstanding questions that the IAEA has about Iran's PMD, possible military dimension, that Iran refuses to provide answers for, giving us more reason to suspect that Iran is pursuing a nuclear program for other than peaceful purposes.

The JPOA sets a bar lower than had previously been established through a series of six U.N. Security Council resolutions. For a nation that has operated a covert nuclear program for decades and which continues to stonewall the most serious inquiries from the IAEA, we should have every reason to suspect that its activities extend further than what has been declared to date.

Just a few weeks ago, it was reported that there may indeed be other covert sites that Iran has not previously declared and this is why this nuclear deal is setting up to be a bad and dangerous deal because it relies on something we cannot guarantee. The only way that we can ensure that Iran is in compliance with the IAEA obligations and is not paving the way toward a nuclear weapon is to fully dismantle its infrastructure because as long as that infrastructure is intact, Iran will always be able to make the decision to go for the bomb and the IAEA or our Intelligence Community does not have the ability, despite what President Obama guarantees, to detect it in time. Shame on us.

And with that, I am glad to yield for his opening statement to my good friend from Florida, the ranking member, Mr. Deutch.

Mr. DEUTCH. Thank you, Madam Chairman. We are now a week away from the deadline to reach a political framework agreement in the negotiations between Iran and the P5+1 over Iran's illicit nuclear program. For all the talk about various elements of a potential deal, including future verification and monitoring, it has been easy to lose sight of a very clear and very current indicator of Iran's willingness to comply with international obligations. That is, its repeated stonewalling and noncompliance with the International Atomic Energy Agency.

The IAEA first found Iran to be in noncompliance with its obligations as a member of the Nuclear Non-Proliferation Treaty in 2005. Between 2005 and 2010, the IAEA issued 30 reports detailing concerns about Iran's activities, ultimately leading to referral to the Security Council and successive rounds of sanctions, including U.N. Security Council resolutions demanding that Iran stop enrichment.

Running parallel to the current P5+1 negotiations, the IAEA, arguably the agency that will be charged with carrying out future monitoring and verification of a nuclear deal, has been engaged in a new round of discussions with Iran. On November 11, 2013, the IAEA and Iran signed a joint statement on a framework for cooperation. In the framework for cooperation, the IAEA and Iran agreed to cooperate further with respect to verification activities to resolve all present and past issues.

In its latest report, on February 19, 2015, the IAEA confirmed that it has only been able to make progress on 1 out of 12 key issues. The report states and I quote,

> "Iran has not provided any explanations that enable the Agency to clarify the two outstanding practical measures nor has it proposed any new practical measures in the next step of the framework for cooperation."

As it has for years, Iran has been slow walking investigations and inspections, refusing to cooperate on providing past activities and refusing access to various suspect sites. And this is simply to carry out its obligations as a member of the Nuclear Non-Proliferation Treaty. There are many of us who fear that this is an unfortunate foreshadowing of the way in which Iran will respond to its obligations should there be a permanent nuclear deal that is reached.

Now if Iran wants to show the world that it can act in good faith or that we should have any belief at all that this regime could be trusted in the future, it would start by cooperating with IAEA. If Iran at the end of any nuclear deal wants to be treated like any other NPT country, it could start by acting like one now.

Extremely concerning throughout this whole process is the refusal to allow IAEA inspectors to certain suspect sites, notably Parchin. With respect to Parchin, as previously reported by the IAEA, the activities that have taken place at this location since

February 2012 are likely to have undermined the Agency's ability to conduct effective verification. It remains important for Iran to provide answers to the Agency's questions and access to the particular location at this site.

But most concerning is Iran's refusal to cooperate on the possible military dimensions of its program. How can we construct a viable verification regime going forward if we don't know fully what the Iranians have done in the past with respect to weaponization? Just this week, speaking at a conference, IAEA Director General Amano stated and I quote,

> "We are also implementing the Joint Plan of Action and we can also say the implementation is good. But with respect to the clarification of issues with possible military dimensions, the progress is limited and this is the area where more cooperation from Iran is needed."

Amano said the Agency still was not able to conclude whether all nuclear material in Iran was being used for peaceful purposes, saying,

> "We continue to verify the nondivergence of nuclear material declared by Iran, but we are still not in a position to conclude that all nuclear material in Iran is peaceful in purpose."

Given Iran's intransigence, the international community is left with little choice but to believe that it has something to hide. And I for one would not be comfortable with any nuclear agreement that doesn't force Iran to come clean on its past activities.

As former IAEA official Olli Heinonen wrote earlier this month,

> "The IAEA can only return to routine inspections when the IAEA is certain that all nuclear material and activities are being used exclusively for peaceful purposes."

And I frankly don't know how we can ever be certain of this when we don't know everything that Iran has done.

Furthermore, as I mentioned at the outset, it will be the IAEA who will be charged with carrying out verification and monitoring should a deal be reached. It is the IAEA that wants to first observe a violation and then what happens? Do the Iranians stonewall as the international community tries to get additional information? Do they have the opportunity to dispute the IAEA's findings? How long will it take for the IAEA to confirm its finding and report to the P5+1? Who is responsible for determining the penalties if a violation occurs? These are all outstanding questions that will need to be answered before any reasonable country should enter into any agreement with Iran.

Lastly, let me just say I frankly am unclear as to how we can reasonably conclude any permanent agreement with Iran on its nuclear activities if the IAEA is unable to finish its parallel investigation.

I thank the witnesses for being here today and I appreciate their insight and I yield back.

Ms. ROS-LEHTINEN. Thank you very much, Mr. Deutch, for that opening statement.

Mr. Issa of California is recognized.

Mr. ISSA. Thank you, Madam Chair. This is an important hearing. I want to hear some of the specifics about the breakout time, the technical problems, and to the greatest extent possible, some of the areas in which the proposed agreement falls short from an inspection standpoint. I also look forward to hearing Mr. Tobey who has vast background and knowledge and history of where we failed before. We failed with India. We failed with Pakistan. We failed with North Korea. The difference in all of those is expansive view of the world and terrorism that clearly is coming from Iran. If they get a nuke, we will never hear or see the last of it in the region.

Having said that, I want to echo the statements of both the chairman and ranking member. When they talk about a country that cannot be trusted, Iran comes to the top of the list. Since 1979, consistently, year after year, decade after decade, what Iran says and Iran does are different. And therefore, until or unless there is an inspection regime that is verifiable and has been consistently verified before a deal, any expectation that once sanctions are lifted that Iran will suddenly be a new and different Iran are, in fact, sillier than the many turnarounds we saw in Groundhog Day those many years ago. The fact is history does repeat itself. Iran will not keep its promises. And Madam Chair, I want to thank you for this important hearing.

Ms. ROS-LEHTINEN. Thank you very much, Mr. Issa. Mr. Boyle of Pennsylvania.

Mr. BOYLE. Thank you and I am reminded of the saying that the best way to predict future behavior is to look at past behavior. So I am especially interested in this subject matter. I have already read the three witnesses' testimonies and I think that judging Iran's experience with respect to the IAEA is a great way to project future behavior.

I also just want to add following on the last comments that were made by Mr. Issa, it is actually remarkable when you look at humankind over the last 65 years that nuclear weaponization has been contained to the extent that it has. The challenge of Iran reaching a nuclear capability is would that be the catalyst to touch off Saudi Arabia and every other regional player also deciding that they would suddenly be interested in this capability.

So with only a minute, I will save the rest of my comments for question time. I would just say I thank the chair and the ranking member for having this incredibly important hearing.

Ms. ROS-LEHTINEN. Thank you, sir. Mr. DeSantis of Florida.

Mr. DESANTIS. Thank you, Madam Chairman. I think a lot of Americans are wondering what is going on with these negotiations. Iran does cheat. Can we trust them? And then lo and behold, a couple of days ago, you have the Supreme Leader, the only decision maker that really matters chanting ''Death to America.'' So is he saying ''Death to America'' because he means it? If so, why would we be negotiating? If he doesn't mean it, how do we trust what he says? It is interesting how that was dismissed by the White House as oh, just mere domestic political rhetoric. Don't worry about that. But when the Prime Minister of Israel says something in the heat of the campaign and then explains, no, you have got to hold him to that. You are going to take him to the United Nations now. We are going to turn our back on Israel.

The national intelligence estimate has removed Iran and Hezbollah as terrorist threats in their recent worldwide threat assessment. Gulf States are responding to the potential for this deal in a way that they clearly don't have confidence in. The Socialist President of France is stronger on Iran than the U.S. administration is right now.

I look forward to the testimony, but I think I speak for a lot of my constituents that we are concerned about this deal.

Ms. ROS-LEHTINEN. Thank you very much, Mr. DeSantis. From Florida also, Mr. Clawson.

Mr. CLAWSON. Thank you for coming. Years ago, there was a movie called Animal House and the characters went on a road trip. You all probably remember the movie. And the character that needed to supply the vehicle was named Flounder. And it was his older brother's shiny black Lincoln Mercury. And so his crazy fraternity brothers wanted to use that car for their road trip. Now he knew he shouldn't have given him the keys. Everybody watching the movie knew he shouldn't give him the keys, that it was going to be a bad outcome. We all knew it. And yet, he gave the keys to his brother's car and of course, they took the car and trashed the car. And at some point afterwards they said ''Flounder, you messed up'' or something to that effect. ''You trusted us.''

We all know if we give the keys, the nuclear keys to Iran, that we are going to look back and say we really messed this up. We trusted them. And so I echo what has already been said here today. I don't know what reason we would have to trust and we all know if we give the nuclear keys to these folks that we are going to regret it. Thank you for coming today.

Ms. ROS-LEHTINEN. Thank you so much, Mr. Clawson. Ms. Frankel.

Ms. FRANKEL. Thank you, Madam Chair, and I may be a little repetitive, but there are three points that I am interested in. First of all, thank you all for being here.

Number one is how confident are you that we would be able to verify a complete Iranian compliance with an interim agreement? Number two, what lessons should we learn from our history with North Korea? And finally, do you have an opinion as to whether a comprehensive agreement should require Iran to come clean on its entire nuclear program including weaponization? And I waive the rest of my time, Madam Chair.

Ms. ROS-LEHTINEN. Those were excellent questions. Thank you so much, Ms. Frankel.

And now we will turn to our witnesses. Thank you very much for being here with us. We are pleased to welcome Mr. William Tobey. He is a senior fellow at the Harvard Kennedy School's Belfer Center for Science and International Affairs. Previously, he was Deputy Administrator for the Defense Nuclear Non-Proliferation at the National Nuclear Security Administration and has served in the National Security Council staff. Welcome, Mr. Tobey.

Second, we welcome Ms. Rebeccah Heinrichs. She is a fellow at the George C. Marshall Institute where she has concentrated her research in the areas of nuclear deterrence and missile defense. She has also held fellowships from The Heritage Foundation, the

7

Foundation for Defense of Democracies, and has previous work as a congressional staffer. Do we pronounce the S in the last name?

Ms. HEINRICHS. Yes.

Ms. ROS-LEHTINEN. Thank you. And last, but certainly not least, we welcome back Mr. David Albright, founder and president of the Institute for Science and International Security. He has authored numerous assessments on covert nuclear weapons programs throughout the world, as well as regular publications on scientific research.

We welcome all of you. Your prepared remarks will be made a part of the record. And Mr. Tobey, you will be recognized after that great intro from Mr. Issa, Mr. Historian.

STATEMENT OF MR. WILLIAM H. TOBEY, SENIOR FELLOW, BELFER CENTER FOR SCIENCE AND INTERNATIONAL AFFAIRS, JOHN F. KENNEDY SCHOOL OF GOVERNMENT, HARVARD UNIVERSITY

Mr. TOBEY. Thank you, Chairman Ros-Lehtinen, Ranking Member Deutch, and members of the committee. It is a pleasure to be here to speak about a matter of surpassing importance.

Preventing Iran from obtaining a nuclear weapon is vital to U.S. national security interest. The committee has asked to focus today on Iran's non-compliance with its safeguards obligations and from the opening statements, it is already clear that the committee has a profound understanding of those issues. So I will confine my remarks to just three points.

First, in 2005, the International Atomic Energy Agency's Board of Governors found that Iran had violated its safeguards obligations by failing in a number of instances over an extended period of time to make necessary declarations.

Second, since 2011, the International Atomic Energy Agency's Secretariat has expressed serious concerns about the possible military dimensions to Iran's nuclear program which Tehran refuses to clarify despite being required to do so under the Joint Plan of Action agreement. And here I would note that many of the members referred to the so-called possible military dimensions and I think that gets to the heart of the important issues on the Iran agreement.

Third, in August 2014, less than 6 months ago, the United States Department of State sanctioned an Iranian Government organization for ongoing nuclear weapons development work.

In sum, Iran has violated its safeguards obligations in the past. It is charged by the United States Government with doing so in the present. And evinces little reason to believe that it will not continue to do so in the future. Thank you.

[The prepared statement of Mr. Tobey follows:]

William H. Tobey
Senior fellow, Belfer Center for Science and International Affairs
John F. Kennedy School of Government
Harvard University
Testimony before the House Foreign Affairs Committee
Subcommittee on the Middle East and North Africa
"Iran's Noncompliance with its International Atomic Energy Agency Obligations"
March 24, 2015

Chairman Ros-Lehtinen, Ranking member Deutch, members of the Committee, it is a pleasure to testify today on a matter of surpassing importance.

Preventing Iran from obtaining nuclear weapons is vital to U.S. national security interests. A key aspect of that matter is Iran's compliance with its Safeguards Agreement with the International Atomic Energy Agency (IAEA) and with other related agreements. It is a broad subject, but I understand the Committee has specific interests, so I will confine my statement to those topics.

History of noncompliance with IAEA Safeguards

Almost ten years ago, on September 24, 2005, the International Atomic Energy Agency Board of Governors first concluded that Iran had violated its Safeguards Agreement. Citing:

> "Iran's failures in a number of instances over an extended period of time to meet its obligations under its NPT Safeguards Agreement (INFCIRC 214) with respect to the reporting of nuclear material, its processing and its use, as well as the declaration of facilities where such material had been processed and stored . . . ."

the Board found:

> "[T]hat Iran's many failures and breaches of its obligations to comply with its NPT Safeguards Agreement . . . constitute noncompliance in the context of Article XII.C of the Agency's Statute . . ."

And, further that:

> "[T]he nature of these activities, issues brought to light in the course of the Agency's verification of the history of concealment of Iran's nuclear activities referred to in the Director General's report, declarations made by Iran since September 2002 and the resulting absence of confidence that Iran's nuclear programme is exclusively for peaceful purposes have given rise to questions that are within the competence of the Security Council . . . ."

The United Nations Security Council affirmed the Board of Governors' position by passing six resolutions on the matter.

On February 18, 2010, an IAEA Secretariat reported to the Board of Governors additional instances of Iranian noncompliance:

> "Both in the case of the Darkhovin facility and the FFEP, Iran did not notify the Agency in a timely manner of the decision to construct or to authorize construction of the facilities, as required in the modified code 3.1, and has provided only limited design information. Iran's actions in this regard are inconsistent with the Subsidiary Arrangements to its Safeguards Agreement, and raise concerns about the completeness of its declarations."

With this bland statement, the IAEA charged Iran with attempting to build a covert enrichment facility, which had been revealed five months earlier, at the time of a United Nations Security Council meeting at the heads-of-state level.

Currently outstanding compliance issues and implications for the P5+1 negotiations

The IAEA has also worked patiently for years to document Iran's clandestine nuclear weapons efforts. Justifiably cautious and analytically rigorous, the Agency calls these the "possible military dimensions" of the Iranian nuclear program and reported on them in detail on November 8, 2011. That anodyne term encompasses 12 sets of activities, most of which can only be explained as efforts to build nuclear weapons, including:

- military leadership of the program;
- clandestine nuclear material acquisition;
- work on "nuclear components for an explosive device";
- "detonator development";
- "hydrodynamic experiments" which test nuclear weapons designs;
- "integration into a missile delivery vehicle"; and,
- work on a "fuzing, arming, and firing system."

The latest report on Safeguards implementation in Iran states, "The Agency has obtained more information since November 2011 that has further corroborated the analysis contained in that Annex." Importantly, the IAEA also uncovered work related to "the development of a nuclear explosive device that continued after 2003." In 2011, IAEA Director General Yukiya Amano said, "The activities in Iran related to the possible military dimension seem to have… continued until quite recently."

Peaceful programs to produce energy or medical isotopes have no use for such work. Tehran denies the agency's charges, but refuses to provide the information necessary to resolve them.

A White House Fact Sheet on the Joint Plan of Action, dated November 23, 2013, stated that,

> "The set of understandings also includes an acknowledgment by Iran that it must address all United Nations Security Council resolutions – which Iran has long claimed are illegal – as well as past and present issues with Iran's nuclear program that have been identified by the International Atomic Energy Agency (IAEA). This would include resolution of questions concerning the possible military dimension of Iran's nuclear program, including Iran's activities at Parchin."

The language of the Joint Plan of Action on the matter is far less specific. It notes only that, "There would be additional steps in between the initial measures and the final step, including, among other things, addressing the UN Security Council resolutions . . . ."

To pursue this matter under the Joint Plan of Action, the IAEA proposed dealing with several issues at first. Despite repeated efforts over a year and a half, on February 19, 2015, the IAEA reported that, "Iran has not provided any explanations that enable the Agency to clarify the two outstanding practical measures relating to the initiation of high explosives and to neutron transport calculations." Worse, the IAEA also reported "activities that have taken place at [Parchin] since February 2012 are likely to have undermined the Agency's ability to conduct effective verification."

Thus, the "possible military dimensions" of Iran's nuclear program remain unresolved and Iran is either not cooperating with, or is actively working against, IAEA efforts to investigate them. Iran is therefore also not complying with the Joint Plan of Action—at least as explained by the White House fact sheet.

According to the IAEA, verifying the scope of the possible military dimensions of Iran's nuclear program "will involve considering and acquiring an understanding of each issue in turn, and then integrating all of the issues into a 'system' and assessing that system as a whole."

This issue rests at the heart of verifying any future agreement, because monitoring would be futile without a full understanding of Iran's past actions. It is not merely a matter of the past, but of the present and future. Unless it is known *who* did *what where* and *when*, it will be impossible to verify that these activities are not recurring. As one unnamed American official explained to the *New York Times* on March 15, 2015, "The issue is deeper than whether you make them admit what they did in the past. It's getting to know their entire scientific infrastructure so you will detect any effort to start up weapons design years from now."

Moreover, these issues must be resolved before a final agreement is reached, or Iran will feel no obligation to provide complete and correct information. If the "possible military dimensions" are not resolved before an agreement, then the IAEA's ability to verify Iran's declarations will be undermined, probably fatally.

The U.S. government also recently charged that Iran is currently pursuing activities inconsistent with its IAEA Safeguards Agreement. On August 29, 2014, the State Department announced additional sanctions against individuals and organizations in Iran. According to the Department, the Organization of Defensive Innovation and Research (known by the acronym SPND) "is primarily responsible for research in the field of nuclear weapons development." The State Department alleges that, "SPND was established in February 2011 by the UN-sanctioned individual Mohsen Fakhrizadeh, who for many years has managed activities useful in the development of a nuclear explosive device." According to the language of the press release, this work is ongoing. Such announcements are not casually written. Interagency teams carefully review them to ensure their accuracy and consistency with law, and that they do not reveal intelligence information or sources and methods.

Reports of additional undisclosed covert sites

On February 24, 2015, the National Council of Resistance of Iran issued a report alleging that Iran maintains a covert site for research and development of advanced uranium enrichment centrifuges. While this is understandably a matter of interest to the Committee, I have no independent means to verify the truth or falsehood of this charge.

The Importance of Verification

Iran's failure to comply with its Safeguards obligations highlights the critical importance of verification in a future agreement. We cannot trust, but we must verify. This will require monitoring of people, sites, and procurement activities designed to ensure that the "possible military dimensions" of Iran's nuclear program identified by the IAEA have ceased and that they do not recur. Also, because the Administration has reportedly chosen accede to Tehran's demands that it retain large centrifuge enrichment operations, it will be necessary to monitor comprehensively production and imports of related materials and equipment to ensure that they are not diverted to a covert effort. This would require verification measures substantially more comprehensive than IAEA Safeguards and the Additional Protocol.

Summary

The IAEA Board of Governors found in 2005 that Iran violated its Safeguards obligations by failing in a number of instances over an extended period of time to make necessary declarations. The IAEA Secretariat has expressed "serious concerns" about "possible military dimensions" to Iran's nuclear program (i.e. nuclear weapons development work), which Tehran has refused to clarify, despite the White House's claim that Iran is required to do so by the Joint Plan of Action. The Agency has further stated that Iran appears to be taking actions that undermine its ability to conduct effective verification. The U.S.

Department of State recently charged an Iranian government organization with ongoing nuclear weapons development work.

In sum, Iran violated its Safeguards obligations in the past, is charged by the U.S. government with doing so in the present, and evinces little reason to believe it will not continue to do so in the future.

Ms. Ros-Lehtinen. Thank you very much, Mr. Tobey. Ms. Heinrichs.

STATEMENT OF MS. REBECCAH L. HEINRICHS, FELLOW, GEORGE C. MARSHALL INSTITUTE

Ms. Heinrichs. Madam Chairman, Ranking Member Deutch, members of the committee, thank you for the invitation to participate in this hearing.

I have spent the last 10 years in various capacities from working for the Congress to working as a researcher in think tanks studying specifically how the U.S. can deter the most catastrophic kinds of attack with an emphasis in ballistic missile defense which is critical should deterrence fail.

Arms control is just one tool for deterring the spread of strategic weapons, but for it to be effective as President Obama said in his 2009 Prague speech, ''Rules must be binding. Violations must be punished. Words must mean something.'' Administration officials have said that Iran cannot be permitted to achieve a nuclear weapons capability which if it did, would be in violation of the NPT as well as several Security Council resolutions, but to allow Iran to maintain its ability to produce a nuclear weapon while also relieving sanctions would signal to foes that violations, if persistent enough, could end in reward.

It is important to keep at the front of our mind the context of which the P5+1 has attempted to secure a diplomatic solution. Iran views the U.S. and Israel as its principal enemies and over the past three decades Iran has very intentionally created a network of terrorist surrogates, able to target U.S. interests and Israel. The regime does not view the P5+1 talks as an opportunity to reconcile with the West. To the contrary, Iran has failed to instill confidence in the most optimistic of U.S. diplomats that it is sincere about maintaining a peaceful nuclear program.

At the recent APEC conference, Ambassador Rice said ''The administration holds a distrust and verify policy toward Iran'' an important twist on President Reagan's policy toward the former Soviet Union, ''Trust, but verify.''

But Iran to this day stonewalls the IAEA's efforts to verify the Iranians' claim that the nuclear program is exclusively for peaceful purposes, making verification nearly impossible.

In 2011, in November, the IAEA laid out possible military dimensions of the program. The Agency concluded that Iran had been undergoing a structured program that included possible weaponization activities until the end of 2003, but then went on to cite activities related to the development of a nuclear explosive device that continued after 2003 and noted that these particular activities could remain ongoing.

And just last month, the IAEA report confirmed again that Iran still has not provided any explanation that enable the Agency to clarify the outstanding practical measures.

But even if the Agency were permitted unfettered access to Iran's scientists, documents, and facilities, and able to get to the bottom of Iran's weaponization activities, by all accounts the negotiations do not include Iran's missile program. Iran wants more than a nuclear weapon. Iran wants to be able to credibly threaten its adversaries with a nuclear armed missile and also with a variety of conventionally armed missiles. The DNI assessed that Iran would likely choose a ballistic missile as its preferred method of delivering a nuclear weapon, if one is ever fielded.

Missiles are a cost effective way for a country like Iran to pose an asymmetric threat to much more militarily sophisticated countries like the U.S., therefore, Iran is motivated to keep and improve his arsenal and has defied U.N. Resolution 1929 in order to do it. For example, it is improving its accuracy of missiles to threaten ships in the Persian Gulf and the Strait of Hormuz and is on a determined course to achieve an intercontinental ballistic missile capable to threaten the U.S. homeland.

Under Secretary of State Wendy Sherman, seeming to back away from her previous commitments to include Iran's missile program before this committee, said that a comprehensive agreement, although it is important to address that Resolution 1929 is ''not about ballistic missiles per se'' but about nuclear arms missiles. But a ballistic missile can carry conventional or a non-conventional warhead including those that are chemical, biological, and nuclear.

In closing, Iran continues to support terrorism and there is no evidence that it has made the political decision to move away from achieving a nuclear weapons capability. Getting to the bottom of what the IAEA identified as the possible military dimensions of Iran's nuclear program ought to be a necessary condition to moving forward with any kind of real negotiations. But even if this is accomplished, any deal focused on Iran's nuclear program must include its missile program. Thank you.

[The prepared statement of Ms. Heinrichs follows:]

Statement of Ms. Rebeccah L. Heinrichs
Fellow, George C. Marshall Institute
"Iran's Noncompliance with Its International Atomic Energy Agency Obligations"
House Foreign Affairs Committee
Subcommittee on The Middle East and North Africa
Tuesday, March 24, 2015
2:00 p.m. -- 2172 Rayburn House Office Building

Chairman Ros-Lehtinen, Ranking Member Deutch, members of the committee, thank you for the invitation to participate in this hearing.

It is important to keep at the front of our minds the context of which the P5+1 has attempted to secure a diplomatic solution to Iran's nuclear program. Iran views the U.S. and Israel as its principal enemies[1] and over the past three decades Iran has very intentionally created a network of terrorist surrogates able to target U.S. interests and Israel.[2]

The terror or militant groups it supports are HAMAS, Lebanese Hezbollah, the Palestinian Islamic Jihad, the Taliban, and Iraqi Shia groups. Hezbollah, in particular, has increased its global terrorist activities to a level greater than the intelligence community has seen since the 1990s.[3]

Iran continues to undermine U.S. interests and that of our allies while expanding its own influence throughout the Middle East. It has done so by exploiting sectarian turmoil and by arming Palestinian groups, Shia (Huthi) rebels in Yemen, and Shia militants in Bahrain, to name just a few.

It is also directly and recently responsible for the death of American soldiers. In 2010, the U.S. Ambassador to Iraq James Jeffrey estimated that groups backed by Iran were responsible for up to a quarter of U.S. deaths in Iraq.[4]

All this to say, the regime does not view the P5+1 talks as an opportunity for rapprochement. To the contrary, it remains committed to its revolutionary objectives, supports terrorism, continues to view the United States as a principal enemy, and has shown unwavering commitment to its illicit programs at enormous cost to its economy and international standing.

---

[1] James Clapper, Director of National Intelligence, Testimony on the U.S. Intelligence Community Worldwide Threat Assessment, Senate Select Committee on Intelligence, March 12, 2013.
[2] Department of Defense, Annual Report on the Military Power of Iran, 2012, accessed online at https://fas.org/man/eprint/dod-iran.pdf
[3] Ibid
[4] Michael Christie, "Quarter of U.S. Deaths Due to Iran Groups-Envoy," Reuters, August 26, 2010.

IAEA CONCERNS REGARDING NUCLEAR PROGRAM

Iran has failed to instill confidence in the most optimistic of U.S. diplomats that it is earnest about maintaining a nuclear program that is exclusively and verifiably for peaceful purposes. At the recent AIPAC conference, National Security Adviser Susan Rice said the administration holds a "distrust yet verify" policy towards Iran, an important twist on President Reagan's policy towards the former Soviet Union: "trust but verify."

But if the U.S. enters negotiations already admitting such distrust, it must be that much more demanding about the verification regime and the cooperation of the Iranians. But the Iranians have not shown a willingness to cooperate. Indeed, during the course of talks Iran has moved forward with what it claims is a peaceful nuclear program in violation of U.N. Security Council resolutions, and has to this day stonewalled the International Atomic Energy Agency's (IAEA) efforts to verify the Iranians' claim that the nuclear program is exclusively for peaceful purposes.

The refusal to fully cooperate with IAEA inspectors has been ongoing for more than a decade.

After the 2002 public disclosure of secret Iranian facilities including the large uranium enrichment plant at Natanz and the Arak heavy water plant, the IAEA began investigating whether or not Iran was in breach of its safeguards agreement and concluded on September 24, 2005 that it was.[5] In the following years the U.N. passed six Security Council resolutions related to its nuclear program.

Rather than cooperating with the IAEA to address the concerns, Iran deceived and blocked inspectors while continuing its program. For example, Iran continued to construct an enrichment facility at Qom violating Security Council calls to suspend all enrichment-related activities, and then did not notify the IAEA of its existence until September 2009.[6]

In November 2011 the IAEA laid out possible military dimensions of the program. The Agency concluded that Iran had been undergoing a "structured program" that included possible weaponization activities until the end of 2003.[7] (In 2007 the Intelligence Community assessed that Ian had suspended its nuclear weapons program in 2003.[8]) The 2011 IAEA report cited activities related to "the development of a nuclear explosive device that continued after 2003" and noted these particular activities could remain ongoing.[9]

---

[5] Implementation of the IAEA Safeguards Agreement in the Islamic Republic of Iran. Resolution adopted by the IAEA Board of Governors, September 24, 2005, (GOV/2005/77).

[6] U.N. Security Council Resolution 1929, adopted June 9, 2010.

[7] Implementation of the NPT Safeguards Agreement and relevant provisions of Security Council resolutions in the Islamic Republic of Iran. Report by the IAEA Director General, November 8, 2011.

[8] Office of the Director of Intelligence, National Intelligence Estimate, Iran: Nuclear Intentions and Capabilities, 2007.

[9] Implementation of the NPT Safeguards Agreement and relevant provisions of Security Council resolutions in the Islamic Republic of Iran. Report by the IAEA Director General, November 8, 2011.

A 2012 resolution adopted by the IAEA confirmed Iran remained uncooperative, had not provided the Agency necessary access to sites requested, in particular the military site Parchin,[10] and was therefore unable to verify that Iran's nuclear program was peaceful. The IAEA's ability to make this verification must be a prerequisite to any deal that could result in advantaging the Iranian regime.

But, in a 2013 public event at the Wilson Center while speaking of the still unaddressed military dimensions of the program, IAEA Director General Yukiya Amano explained that getting to the bottom of the concerns was an effort ongoing in parallel with the P5+1 talks, but emphasized that "it is essential that Iran cooperate with us to clarify these issues."[11]

Days before the November 24, 2014 political framework deadline Mr. Amano told the agency's board of governors, "Iran has not provided any explanations that enable the Agency to clarify the outstanding practical measures, nor has it proposed any new practical measures in the next step of the Framework for Cooperation, despite several requests from the Agency."[12]

Just last month, an IAEA report again confirmed that "Iran has not provided any explanations that enable the agency to clarify the outstanding practical measures."[13]

IRAN'S MISSILE PROGRAM

By all accounts, the P5+1 talks have focused on narrow portions of the nuclear program to the exclusion of other issues, including Iran's missile program. Iran wants more than a nuclear weapon. It wants to be able to credibly threaten its adversaries with a nuclear-armed missile, and also with a variety of conventionally armed missiles.

U.N. Security Council Resolution 1929 explicitly seeks to curb Iran's missile program. It plainly states: "Iran shall not undertake any activity related to ballistic missiles capable of delivering nuclear weapons, including launches using ballistic missile technology, and that States shall take all necessary measures to prevent the transfer of technology or technical assistance to Iran related to such activities."[14]

Missiles are a cost-effective way for a country like Iran to pose an asymmetric threat to much more militarily sophisticated countries like the U.S. and are powerful weapons for coercion; therefore, Iran is motivated to keep and improve its arsenal. Indeed, Iran has the region's largest arsenal of ballistic missiles and is developing their quality at a rate faster than previously thought.[15] Its arsenal includes conventional ballistic missiles, anti-ship ballistic missiles, cruise

---

[10]Implementation of the NPT Safeguards Agreement and relevant provisions of Security Council resolutions in the Islamic Republic of Iran, IAEA Board of Governors, September 13, 2012.

[11] Transcript from a public event with Mr. Yukiya Amano at the Wilson Center, November 6, 2013, at http://www.wilsoncenter.org/sites/default/files/amanoevent_transcript.pdf.

[12] Jeremy Diamond, International Nuclear Watchdog: Iran Needs to Cooperate. CNN, November 20, 2014.

[13] Shadia Nasralla, Iran Still Stalling U.N. Nuclear Inquiry as Deal Deadline Looms: IAEA, Reuters, February 19, 2015.

[14] U.N. Security Council Resolution 1929, adopted on June 9, 2010.

[15] General Charles H. Jacoby, Jr., Commander of Northern Command, statement before the House Armed Services Committee, February 26, 2014.

missiles, and surface-to-air (SAM) missiles. Notably, Iran has flight-tested its Fateh-110 ballistic missile, and by modifying it, improved its accuracy giving it the ability to threaten ships in the Persian Gulf and the Strait of Hormuz.[16] Iran has continued its intercontinental ballistic missile (ICBM) development, which if achieved would give it the ability to threaten the United States homeland. Iran has used its long-range rockets to orbit satellites in 2009, 2011, 2012, and again on February 2, 2015 of this year.[17] Satellite launches possess technologies directly relevant to the development of ICBMs.[18] Intelligence reports have consistently assessed that with foreign assistance Iran could have the ability to flight-test an ICBM by 2015.[19]

Additionally, in February 2014, the Iranian military announced it had successfully tested an indigenously produced long-range missile. It is worth noting that the missile tests occurred on the eve of the 35th anniversary of the Islamic Revolution, showing the importance Iran places the advancement of its missile program within the context of its larger strategic objectives. Celebrating the revolution Iranian President Hassan Rouhani said, "The revolution started because people didn't want to accept humiliation," Rouhani told his country. "Is it possible for the great revolutionary people, it is possible for this nation to accept humiliation by foreign powers or America after 35 years? It is as if they have not recognized the great nation of Iran..."[20]

The 2013 Worldwide Threats report by the Director of National Intelligence assessed "We judge Iran would likely choose a ballistic missile as its preferred method of delivering a nuclear weapon, if one is ever fielded."[21]

According to press reports, over the summer Mr. Khamenei called on the IRGC to mass-produce ballistic missiles.[22] Surprising no one, the head of Iran's Islamic Revolutionary Guard Corps Aerospace-Force said his country's "defense capabilities, specifically its ballistic missiles, are non-negotiable.[23]

During a Senate Foreign Relations Committee hearing in February 2014 Undersecretary of State for Political Affairs Wendy Sherman stated that the current negotiations with Iran, "does address the fact that their ballistic missiles that could be used as a delivery mechanism for nuclear weapons must be addressed as part of a comprehensive solution because it is part of the U.N. Security Council resolutions. So it is true that in these first six months we have not shut down all of their production of any ballistic missile that could have anything to do with delivery of a

---

[16] Vice Admiral James Syring, testimony before the House Armed Services, Subcommittee on Strategic Forces, March 25, 2014.

[17] Stephen Clark, "Iranian Satellite Successfully Placed in Orbit," *Spaceflight Now*, February 2, 2015.

[18] General Charles H. Jacoby, Jr., Commander of Northern Command, Northern Command posture statement before the House Armed Services Committee, February 26, 2014.

[19] U.S. Department of Defense, *Report on Military Power of Iran*, January 2014.

[20] Holly Yan, "Iran Touts Launch of New Missiles; U.S. Says Its Watching Closely," CNN.com, February 11, 2014.

[21] James Clapper, Director of National Intelligence, "U.S. Intelligence Community Worldwide Threat Assessment Statement for the Record," March 12, 2013.

[22] "Iran Makes the Rules," *The Wall Street Journal*, September 29, 2014.

[23] Behnam Ben Taleblu, Patrick Megahan, "Iran Fires Cruise Missile Through Sanctions Loophole." Foundation for Defense of Democracies, March 11, 2015.

nuclear weapon, but that is, indeed, going to be part of something that has to be addressed as part of a comprehensive agreement."[24]

Then, in a July 2014 hearing with this Committee, Undersecretary Sherman, seeming to back away from her earlier contention that the Iranian ballistic missile program will be included in a comprehensive agreement, remarked that Resolution 1929 is "not about ballistic missiles per se," but about nuclear-armed missiles.[25]

But, a ballistic missile can carry a conventional or non-conventional warhead including those that are chemical, biological, and nuclear.[26]

Iran continues to support terrorism and there is no evidence that it has made the political decision to move away from achieving a nuclear weapons capability. Any deal that purports to stop its program must have stringent verification measures and Iran must be required to fully cooperate with the IAEA. Getting to the bottom of the possible military dimensions of Iran's nuclear program ought to be a necessary condition to moving forward with any kind of negotiations. Even if this is accomplished, any deal focused on Iran's nuclear program must include its formidable missile program.

Thank you again for the invitation to discuss this subject. I look forward to your questions.

---

[24] Oral testimony from Undersecretary of State Wendy Sherman before the Senate Foreign Relations Committee on the "Iran Nuclear Negotiations," February 4, 2014.
[25] Hearing before the House Foreign Affairs Committee, July 29, 2014.
[26] Ballistic and Cruise Missile Threat. National Air and Space Intelligence Center, 2013.

Ms. Ros-Lehtinen. Thank you very much. Mr. Albright.

STATEMENT OF MR. DAVID ALBRIGHT, FOUNDER AND PRESIDENT, INSTITUTE FOR SCIENCE AND INTERNATIONAL SECURITY

Mr. Albright. Thank you, Madam Chairman, Ranking Member Deutch and other members. Thank you for inviting me to testify today.

Adequate verification is critical to a long term nuclear deal with Iran. Robust measures are needed to ensure declared nuclear sites engage in only peaceful activities and more importantly to ensure the absence of undeclared nuclear material and facilities in Iran. Although the interim deal under the JPA strengthen the monitoring of declared nuclear facilities, it did little to increase the IAEA's ability to detect and find covert sites and activities. The IAEA has regularly reported in its quarterly safeguards report on Iran that it is not in the position to provide credible assurance that all nuclear material in Iran is used for peaceful activities.

Whether this situation changes will largely depend on the ability of the United States and its partners to create a long-term agreement that establishes legally binding conditions on Iran that go beyond those in the comprehensive safeguards agreement and the additional protocol. A critical question will be whether the agreement establishes a verification regime adequate to promptly catch Iran in cheating.

There are many reasons why an agreement must require extraordinary verification arrangements as has been pointed out today so far by I guess every speaker. The most critical ones are Iran's well documented violations of its safeguards agreement, its actions inconsistent with that agreement and a peaceful nuclear program and Iran's long history of non-cooperation with the IAEA.

Let me just list a few additional examples. Iran has built several nuclear facilities in secret. It has been pointed out that Iran has violated its comprehensive safeguards agreement prior to 2004 on multiple occasions. Iran has depended extensively on illegal overseas procurements of a range of goods for its nuclear programs in violation of national laws and U.N. Security Council resolutions. At least one illegal procurement for the Arak reactor complex was attempted after the JPOA went into effect. Although this is not a violation of the JPOA, it does violate U.N. Security Council Resolutions.

Iran has not allowed the IAEA to visit the site at Parchin which has been mentioned already or other sites associated with past work on nuclear weapons research and development and other military nuclear activities. Iran has delayed inspectors' access to sites and extensively modified buildings or the sites themselves in apparent efforts to thwart IAEA verification methods. And of course, Iran has stonewalled the IAEA in resolving the inspectors' concerns about the possible military dimensions of Iran's nuclear programs.

This record demonstrates why Iran has a significant confidence deficit with much of the international community. As a result, verification conditions in a long-term deal will need to be rigorous, unprecedented, and long lasting. These extraordinary conditions need to remain in place for at least 20 years. This time frame should be sufficient for the IAEA to achieve full confidence in the absence of undeclared Iranian nuclear materials and facilities and in a peaceful nature of Iran's nuclear programs.

To that end, several measures are needed to ensure adequate verification and a long-term deal. I agree with others, other members, or with members and with my panel that Iran must address the IAEA's concerns about Iran's past and possibly ongoing nuclear weapons research and development. An agreement that sidesteps the military nuclear issues would risk being unverifiable. Moreover, the world would not be so concerned if Iran had never conducted weaponization activities aimed at building a nuclear weapon. If no concrete progress on this issue is forthcoming by July 1st, a deal should not be signed. If Iran in good faith asks to delay demonstrating concrete progress until after a deal is signed, it should not receive any sanctions relief until it fulfills its commitment along with providing a road map on resolving the rest of the IAEA's concerns.

Visits to Parchin and related sites and access to key individuals should be part of Iran's demonstration of concrete progress.

United Nations Security Council sanctions on proliferation-sensitive goods such as dual use high tech goods should be maintained during the duration of the deal. Authorized nuclear programs could be exempted from these sanctions via specially monitored procurement channel. Often overlooked, these sanctions are critical to building an adequate verification regime. These sanctions are a fundamental part of ensuring that Iran is not secretly establishing the wherewithal to build secret nuclear sites, make secret advances in its advanced centrifuge or other nuclear programs or surge in capability if it left the agreement.

And finally, a deal must include legally binding provisions that allow the IAEA to conduct snap inspections or anywhere anytime inspections. These provisions need to also require broader Iranian declarations about nuclear activities than those required in additional protocol. These conditions should also last for at least 20 years.

So thank you very much for the opportunity to testify.

[The prepared statement of Mr. Albright follows:]

Adequate Verification Under a Comprehensive Iran Nuclear Deal

Testimony
Before
the House Subcommittee on the Middle East and North Africa,
Committee on Foreign Affairs

"Iran's Noncompliance with its International Atomic Energy Agency Obligations"

March 24, 2015

By
David Albright
President, Institute for Science and International Security

Difficult-to-bridge differences remain between Iran and the P5+1 group of countries (the United States, Britain, France, Germany, Russia, and China) over a final, comprehensive solution on Iran's nuclear program sought under the November 2013 Joint Plan of Action (JPA). A critical set of issues involves the adequacy of verification arrangements that would be in place to monitor Iran's compliance with the deal. Much of this verification effort will be overseen by the International Atomic Energy Agency (IAEA). The United States has recognized that the current verification arrangements in Iran, namely a comprehensive safeguards agreement (CSA), even if supplemented by the Additional Protocol, are not sufficient in the case of the Islamic Republic of Iran. Tehran's long history of violations, subterfuge, and non-cooperation require extraordinary arrangements to ensure that Iran's nuclear program is indeed peaceful. A priority of the on-going negotiations is establishing legally binding measures guaranteeing this adequate verification.

On a separate but linked negotiating track, Iran and the IAEA have been working in a step-wise approach to address the IAEA's concerns about Iran's alleged past and possibly on-going work on nuclear weapons development and other possible military dimensions (PMD) of Iran's nuclear program. However, this IAEA/Iran track has gone poorly, and Iran has shown increasingly an unwillingness to address the IAEA's concerns. Despite the approaching deadline to come to a comprehensive accord, the Islamic Republic recently denigrated the IAEA's efforts to bring Iran into compliance with its safeguards obligations. Iran's March 11, 2015 official communication regarding the IAEA's most recent quarterly safeguards report showed that the Iranian government continues to dissemble and stonewall the inspectors and remains committed to severely weakening IAEA safeguards and verification in general.[1] Without a fundamental

---

[1] In this communication, Iran rejected several components of the IAEA's investigation as unwarranted. See IAEA Information Circular, "Communication dated 11 March 2015 received from the Permanent Mission of the Islamic

shift in Iran's views on safeguards and verification, the prospect of obtaining adequate verification measures fades.

Adequate verification is critical to a long-term deal in terms of verifying activities at declared nuclear sites and more importantly ensuring the absence of undeclared nuclear material and facilities. Although the interim deal under the JPA strengthened the monitoring of declared sites, it did little to increase the IAEA's ability to detect and find covert sites and activities. Inspectors have regularly reported in quarterly safeguards reports on Iran that the IAEA is not in a position to provide credible assurance about the absence of undeclared nuclear material and activities in Iran, and therefore to conclude that all nuclear material in Iran is used for peaceful activities.

Whether this situation changes will largely depend on the ability of the United States and its partners to create a long term agreement that creates legally binding conditions on Iran that go beyond those in the comprehensive safeguards agreement and the Additional Protocol. A critical question will be whether the agreement establishes a verification regime adequate to promptly catch Iranian cheating.

There are many reasons why an agreement must require extraordinary verification arrangements. The most critical reasons are Iran's violations of its safeguards agreement, actions which have been inconsistent with that agreement and a peaceful nuclear program, and its long history of non-cooperation with the IAEA. Examples include:

- The IAEA found that Iran had violated its comprehensive safeguards agreement prior to 2004 on multiple occasions, including, to name a few, importing natural uranium without notifying the IAEA, enriching uranium to test centrifuges, experimenting with plutonium separation and laser enrichment, and allegedly carrying out weaponization experiments, possibly including nuclear material. (See appendix 1).
- Iran built several nuclear facilities in secret, including the Natanz centrifuge plant, the Fordow centrifuge plant, the Kalaye Electric centrifuge research and development site, the Physics Research Center at Lavisan-Shian linked to undeclared military nuclear work, the Lashkar Ab'ad laser enrichment facility, and the Arak heavy water production plant. In addition, Iran created a secret centrifuge manufacturing complex, parts of which are still secret today.
- Iran has depended extensively on illegal overseas procurement for its nuclear programs in violation of national laws and UN Security Council resolutions; at least one illegal procurement for the Arak reactor complex was attempted after the JPA went into effect (although not a violation of the JPA, it violated UNSC resolutions). (See Appendix 2).
- Iran unilaterally stopped implementing Code 3.1 of its CSA in 2006, an act the IAEA called inconsistent with its safeguards agreement. Code 3.1 of the subsidiary arrangement of the safeguards agreement requires a state to declare a nuclear site when it authorizes or starts to design a nuclear facility and to submit design information as work proceeds.

Republic of Iran to the Agency regarding the Report of the Director General on the Implementation of Safeguards in Iran," INFCIRC/873, March 17, 2015.

- Iran has not allowed the IAEA to visit a site at the Parchin military complex or other sites associated with past work on nuclear weapons research and development and other military nuclear activities.
- Iran has delayed inspectors' access to sites and extensively modified buildings or the sites themselves in apparent efforts to thwart IAEA verification methods which aim to detect undeclared activities and facilities. Iran attempted to prevent these methods from succeeding in 2003 at the Kalaye Electric centrifuge research and development site but was caught; its efforts at sanitization and concealment succeeded at the Lavisan-Shian site, which it bulldozed and rebuilt into an athletic facility after suspicion was raised that it was allegedly involved in military nuclear work; Iran's efforts may yet succeed to conceal from environmental sampling and other verification techniques any past work at the Parchin site where high explosive tests related to nuclear weaponization may have been conducted.
- Iran has stonewalled the IAEA's efforts to resolve its concerns about the possible military dimensions of its nuclear programs. (See Appendix 3).

Iran has in general been in compliance with the conditions of the JPA. However, it enriched in the IR-5 centrifuge, an act inconsistent with its JPA undertakings.[2] When confronted by the United States, Iran quickly backed down and even took additional steps to increase confidence that enrichment in this centrifuge would not happen again. However, Iran has not shown a willingness to back down on more fundamental issues, such as resolving the IAEA's PMD concerns, halting its illicit nuclear procurements, and fully cooperating with the IAEA. On less important issues, Iran is more cooperative but on the difficult ones, its record remains problematic.

Iran has carried out unprecedented violations, both in the length and depth of these violations, and has been non-cooperative with the IAEA and UN Security Council. There is a significant confidence deficit between Iran and much of the international community. As a result, verification conditions in a long term deal will likewise need to be rigorous, unprecedented, and long lasting. These extraordinary conditions need to remain in place for at least twenty years. This time frame should be sufficient for the IAEA to achieve full confidence in the absence of undeclared Iranian nuclear materials and facilities and in the peaceful nature of Iran's nuclear programs.

To that end, several measures are needed to ensure adequate verification in a long term deal:

- Iran addressing the IAEA's concerns about Iran's past and possibly on-going nuclear weapons work. If no concrete progress is forthcoming by July 1, a deal should not be signed. If Iran in good faith asks to delay demonstrating concrete progress until after a deal is signed, it should not receive any sanctions relief until it fulfills this commitment, along with providing a road map on resolving the rest of the IAEA's PMD concerns. Visits to Parchin and related sites and access to key individuals should be part of the demonstration of concrete progress;

---

[2] After enrichment and measurement of enrichment level was achieved, the enriched material and depleted uranium was mixed together, becoming natural uranium.

- Maintenance of United Nations Security Council sanctions on proliferation-sensitive goods during the duration of a deal. These sanctions are a fundamental part of ensuring that Iran is not secretly outfitting undeclared nuclear facilities and activities; and
- Establishment of binding language guaranteeing the IAEA snap inspections, or anywhere, anytime inspections, and broader Iranian declarations about its activities than required in the Additional Protocol, lasting for longer than the reported term of a deal, or about twenty years until the IAEA has satisfactorily concluded its PMD investigation and several more years have passed wherein Iran is compliant with its NPT obligations.

1) Achieve Concrete Progress in Resolving Concerns about Iran's Past and Possibly Ongoing Nuclear Weapons Efforts Prior to Any Sanctions Relief

Despite a great effort over the last year and half, the IAEA has learned little from Iran that has added to the inspectors' ability to resolve its concern about Iran's past and possibly on-going work on nuclear weapons research and development. For years, the inspectors have unsuccessfully asked the Islamic Republic to address the substantial body of evidence that it was developing nuclear weapons prior to 2004 and that it may have continued some of that, or related work, afterwards and even up to the present. Before sanctions are removed, concrete progress is needed on the central issue of whether Iran has worked on nuclear weapons and is maintaining a capability to revive such efforts in the future. A deal also needs to lay out a road map of how and when Iran will address the IAEA's remaining PMD concerns.

Supreme Leader Ali Khamenei often declares that nuclear weapons violate Islamic strictures. His denials are not credible. The United States, its main European allies, and most importantly the IAEA itself, assess that Iran had a sizable nuclear weapons program into 2003. The U.S. intelligence community in the 2007 National Intelligence Estimate (NIE) agreed: "We assess with high confidence that until fall 2003, Iranian military entities were working under government direction to develop nuclear weapons." European governments and the IAEA have made clear, the United States less so, that they believe Iran's nuclear weapons development may have continued after 2003, albeit in a less structured manner. In its November 2011 safeguards report, the IAEA provided evidence of Iran's pre- and post-2003 nuclear weaponization efforts. The IAEA found, "There are also indications that some activities relevant to the development of a nuclear explosive device continued after 2003, and that some may still be ongoing."[3] To reinforce this point to Iran, the United States in late August sanctioned Iran's Organization of Defensive Innovation and Research (SPND), headed by Mohsen Fakrizadeh, the suspected military head of the nuclear weapons program in the early 2000s and perhaps today. SPND is a Tehran-based entity established in early 2011 that is "primarily responsible for research in the field of nuclear weapons development."[4] Thus, there is widespread evidence and suggestion that

---

[3] IAEA Director General, Implementation of the NPT Safeguards Agreement and relevant provisions of Security Council resolutions in the Islamic Republic of Iran, GOV/2011/65, November 8, 2011, Para. 45. http://isis-online.org/uploads/isis-reports/documents/IAEA_Iran_8Nov2011.pdf

[4] U.S. State Department, "Additional Sanctions Imposed by the Department of State Targeting Iranian Proliferators." Media Note, Office of the Spokesperson, Washington, DC, August 29, 2014. http://www.state.gov/r/pa/prs/ps/2014/231159.htm The media note states:

> "SPND was established in February 2011 by the UN-sanctioned individual Mohsen Fakhrizadeh, who for many years has managed activities useful in the development of a nuclear explosive device. Fakhrizadeh led such efforts in the late 1990s or early 2000s, under the auspices of the AMAD Plan, the MODAFL

Iran has worked on developing nuclear weapons and that some of those activities may have continued to today.

Despite the overwhelming evidence, Iran denies it has ever worked on nuclear weapons. Some argue that Iran should not have to confess its past; its face should be saved, they argue. However, making this determination should not be the role of U.S. negotiators. The power to make a determination about Iran's past or ongoing military nuclear work resides with the IAEA. Moreover, emphasizing such an approach emboldens Iran to further resist the IAEA and necessary verification arrangements, ultimately threatening the viability of any deal. If Iran is allowed to "save face" and not address the IAEA's PMD file, it will ultimately be given the ability to maintain the remnants or continued efforts of this military nuclear work, hidden from inspectors and the international community.

Addressing the IAEA's concerns about the military dimensions of Iran's nuclear programs is fundamental to any long-term agreement. Although much of the debate about an agreement with Iran rightly focuses on Tehran's uranium enrichment and plutonium production capabilities, an agreement that side steps the military issues would risk being unverifiable. Moreover, the world would not be so concerned if Iran had never conducted weaponization activities aimed at building a nuclear weapon. After all, Japan has enrichment activities but this program is not regarded with suspicion. The establishment of Iran's peaceful intentions, resting on solid verification procedures, is critical to a serious agreement.

A prerequisite for a comprehensive agreement is for the IAEA to know when Iran sought nuclear weapons, how far it got, what types it sought to develop, and how and where it did this work. Was this weapons capability just put on the shelf, waiting to be quickly restarted? The IAEA needs a good baseline of Iran's military nuclear activities, including the manufacturing of equipment for the program and any weaponization related studies, equipment, and locations. The IAEA needs this information to design a verification regime. Moreover, to develop confidence in the absence of these activities—a central mission—the IAEA will need to periodically inspect these sites and interview key individuals for years to come. Without information about past military nuclear work, it cannot know where to go and who to speak to. The IAEA may require the duration of an agreement to conduct this investigation even with absolute transparency and cooperation on the part of Iran. It would require several more years wherein Iran is compliant with its obligations in order to have confidence in Iran's commitment.

The situation today makes it impossible for the IAEA to determine with confidence that nuclear weapons activities are not on-going. The IAEA already has the legal right to pursue these questions, including accessing military sites, under the comprehensive safeguards agreement with Iran. Despite this right, Iran has refused to allow the IAEA access to military sites. Early in the JPA negotiations, according to U.S. officials involved in the negotiations, Iranian negotiators

---

subsidiary Section for Advanced Development Applications and Technologies (SADAT) and Malek Ashtar University of Technology (MUT). In February 2011, Fakhrizadeh left MUT to establish SPND. Fakhrizadeh was designated in UNSCR 1747 (2007) and by the United States in July 2008 for his involvement in Iran's proscribed WMD activities. SPND took over some of the activities related to Iran's undeclared nuclear program that had previously been carried out by Iran's Physics Research Center, the AMAD Plan, MUT, and SADAT."

said that the Iran Revolutionary Guard Corps would not allow the IAEA access to its military sites. Of course, this demand is unacceptable. Nevertheless, because of Iran's refusal to abide by its safeguards obligations, a long term deal needs to include clear, legally enforceable conditions allowing the IAEA prompt access to military sites where suspicious activities have been detected or reported.

One outstanding case of Iran's refusal to allow access to military sites involves the Parchin military complex. This site is the alleged location of high-explosive testing linked to nuclear weapons development prior to 2004. Since the IAEA asked to visit this site in early 2012, Iran has reconstructed much of it, making IAEA verification efforts all but impossible. Tehran has undertaken at this site what looks to most observers as a blatant effort to defeat IAEA verification. Because of such extensive modifications, the IAEA, once allowed access, may not be able to resolve all its concerns. Undoubtedly, the IAEA will need to visit related sites. A deal should not be signed unless Iran has allowed the IAEA access to Parchin and related sites.

Iran continues to say no to IAEA requests to interview key individuals, such as Fakrizadeh and Sayyed Abbas Shahmoradi-Zavareh, former head of the Physics Research Center, alleged to be the central location in the 1990s of Iran's militarized nuclear research. The IAEA interviewed Shahmoradi years ago about a limited number of his suspicious procurement activities conducted through Sharif University of Technology, at a time when Iran's current head of the Atomic Energy Organization of Iran was head of this university and aware of Shahmoradi's activities. The IAEA was not fully satisfied with his answers and its dissatisfaction increased once he refused to discuss his activities for the Physics Research Center. Since the initial interviews, the IAEA has obtained far more information, some supplied by my institute, about Shahmoradi and the Physics Research Center's procurement efforts.[5] The need to interview both individuals, as well as others, remains.

If Iran is able to successfully evade addressing the IAEA's concerns now, when biting sanctions are in place, why would it address them later when these sanctions are lifted, regardless of anything it may pledge today? Iran's lack of clarity on alleged nuclear weaponization and its noncooperation with the IAEA, if accepted as part of a nuclear agreement, would create a large vulnerability in any future verification regime. Iran would have succeeded in creating precedents to deny inspectors access to key military facilities and individuals. There would be essentially no-go zones across the country for inspectors. Tehran could declare a suspect site a military base and thus off limits. And what better place to conduct clandestine, prohibited activities, such as uranium enrichment and weaponization? After all, the Fordow centrifuge plant was originally built in secret at a military site and only declared to the IAEA after Iran learned it was exposed.

Iran would have also defeated a central tenet of IAEA inspections—the need to determine both the correctness and completeness of a state's nuclear declaration. As Iran's March 11 communication to the IAEA makes clear, Iran actively opposes the IAEA's ability to carry out this well-established mission.

---

5 See for example, Albright, Paul Brannan, and Andrea Stricker, The Physics Research Center and Iran's Parallel Military Nuclear Program, ISIS Report, February 23, 2012. http://isis-online.org/uploads/isis-reports/documents/PHRC_report_23February2012.pdf

Without resolving the PMD issues, the history of Iran's previous military nuclear efforts may never come to light and the international community would lack confidence that these capabilities would not emerge in the future. Moreover, Iran's ratification of the Additional Protocol or acceptance of additional verification conditions, while making the IAEA's verification task easier in several important ways, would not solve the basic problem posed by Iran's lack of cooperation on key, legitimate IAEA concerns. Other countries contemplating the clandestine development of nuclear weapons will certainly watch Tehran closely.

Iran still has plenty of time before July 1, 2015 to address all the IAEA's outstanding PMD concerns. Solving this issue does not require a *mea culpa* from Iran. Numerous approaches have been explored that can provide a mechanism to postpone a potentially embarrassing, albeit needed, admission. A simple acknowledgement of a past military nuclear program would be a positive step, and absent that, a decision not to dispute an IAEA finding on the matter. If no concrete progress is forthcoming by July 1, a deal should not be signed. If Iran in good faith asks to delay demonstrating concrete progress until after a deal is signed, it should not receive any sanctions relief until it fulfills this commitment, along with providing a road map on resolving the rest of the IAEA's PMD concerns. Visits to Parchin and related sites and access to key individuals should be part of the demonstration of concrete progress.

2) Maintain Sanctions on Proliferation Sensitive Goods

An often overlooked aspect of verifying against Iran's construction of secret nuclear sites or any other undeclared activities is preventing Iran's illegal procurements of critical goods and technologies. Iran depends on the foreign acquisition of a wide range of goods for its nuclear programs and has undertaken extensive and elaborate overseas illegal procurements in order to build its nuclear facilities. However, similar to its attitudes toward the IAEA and safeguards, Iran views others' national trade control laws and UN Security Council sanctions with contempt. On August 30, 2014, Iranian President Hassan Rouhani stated on Iranian television: "Of course we bypass sanctions. We are proud that we bypass sanctions." Few, if any, presidents proclaim such pride in conducting internationally illegal activities.

Evidence indicates that in the last few years Iran has been conducting its illegal operations to import goods for its nuclear program with greater secrecy and sophistication, necessitating greater attention to this issue. A long term nuclear agreement should ban Iranian illicit trade in items for its nuclear programs while creating additional mechanisms to verify this ban.

Because of Iran's extensive commitment to smuggling, a long term deal must create a basis to end, or at least detect with high probability, Iran's illicit procurement of goods for its nuclear programs. Such a verified ban is a critical part of ensuring that Iran is not establishing the wherewithal to:

- Build secret nuclear sites,
- Make secret advances in its advanced centrifuge or other nuclear programs, or
- Surge in capability if it left the agreement.

A comprehensive nuclear agreement is not expected to end Iran's illicit efforts to obtain goods for its missile and other military programs. Iran appears committed to continuing its illicit operations to obtain goods for a range of sanctioned programs. Given Iran's sanctions-busting history, a comprehensive nuclear agreement should not include any provisions that would interfere in efforts of the international community to effectively sanction Iranian military programs.

These conditions argue for continuing all the UNSC and national sanctions and well-enforced export controls on proliferation-sensitive goods. Such goods are those key goods used or needed in Iran's nuclear programs and nuclear weapon delivery systems, the latter typically interpreted as covering ballistic missiles.

Sanctions should continue on the listed goods in the UNSC resolutions, many of them dual-use in nature, and more generally on those other dual-use goods that could contribute to uranium enrichment, plutonium reprocessing, heavy water, and nuclear weapon delivery systems (see United Nations Security Council resolution 1929, par. 13). The latter is often referred to as the "catch-all" provision and mirrors many national catch-all requirements in export control laws and regulations. In the case of Iran, this provision is especially important. Without illicitly obtaining the goods covered by catch-all, Iran would be severely constrained in building or expanding nuclear sites.

Verified Procurement Channel for Authorized Nuclear Programs

The six powers must carefully include in any agreement an architecture to mitigate and manage proliferation-related procurement risks. A priority is creating a verifiable procurement channel to route needed goods to Iran's authorized nuclear programs. The agreement will need to allow for imports to legitimate nuclear programs, as they do now for the Bushehr nuclear power reactor.

A challenge will be creating and maintaining an architecture, with a broader nuclear procurement channel, that permits imports of goods to Iran's authorized nuclear programs and possibly later to its civilian industries, while preventing imports to military programs and banned or covert nuclear programs. The UNSC and its Iran sanctions committee and Panel of Experts, the IAEA, and supplier states will all need to play key roles in verifying the end use of exports to Iran's authorized nuclear programs and ensuring that proliferation sensitive goods are not going to banned nuclear activities or military programs.

The creation of the architecture should be accomplished during the negotiations of the long-term deal, although its implementation may need to wait. It will be important that the architecture, whether or not implemented later, be established at the very beginning of the implementation of the long-term agreement in order to adequately deal with this issue.

The reason for creating a verified procurement channel is that Iran's legitimate nuclear activities may need imports. The "modernization" of the Arak reactor would probably involve the most imports, depending on the extent to which international partners are involved. A sensitive area will be any imports, whether equipment, material, or technologies, which are associated with the heavy water portion of the reactor, in the case that the reactor is not converted to light water.

Another sensitive set of possible imports involves goods related to the separation of radionuclides from irradiated targets, although goods for reprocessing, i.e. separating plutonium from irradiated fuel or targets, would be banned since Iran is expected to commit in the long-term agreement not to conduct reprocessing. Nonetheless, allowed imports could include goods that would be close in capability to those used in reprocessing, since the boundary in this area between sensitive and non-sensitive equipment is very thin. These goods will therefore require careful monitoring. Iran's centrifuge program, if reduced in scale to the levels required for U.S. acceptance of a deal, will result in a large excess stockpile of key goods for IR-1 centrifuges. This stock should last for many years, eliminating the need for most imports. Nonetheless, the centrifuge program may need certain spare parts, raw materials, or replacement equipment. If Iran continues centrifuge research and development, that program may require sensitive raw materials and equipment. Needless to say, the goods exported to Iran's centrifuge programs will require careful monitoring as to their use and long term fate.

Iran's non-nuclear civilian industries and institutions may also want to purchase dual-use goods covered by the sanctions, but this sector should not expect to be exempted from sanctions during the duration of the deal or at least until late in the deal. Iran must prove it is fully complying with the agreement and will not abuse a civilian sector exemption to obtain banned goods for its nuclear, missile, or other military programs. With renewed economic activity and as part of efforts to expand the high-tech civilian sector, Iranian companies and institutions engaged in civilian, non-nuclear activities can be expected to seek these goods, several of which would be covered by the catch-all condition of the resolutions. Examples of dual-use goods would be carbon fiber, vacuum pumps, valves, computer control equipment, subcomponents of equipment, and other proliferation sensitive goods. Currently, these civil industries (Iran's petro-chemical and automotive industries are two such examples) are essentially denied many of these goods under the UNSC resolutions and related unilateral and multilateral sanctions. However, if civilian industries are to be eventually exempted from the sanctions, this exemption must be created with special care, implemented no sooner than many years into the agreement, and monitored especially carefully. Iran could exploit this exemption to obtain goods illicitly for banned activities. It could approach suppliers claiming the goods are for civil purposes but in fact they would be for banned nuclear or military programs. Such a strategy is exactly what Iran's nuclear program has pursued illicitly for many years, including cases where goods were procured under false pretenses by the Iranian oil and gas industry for the nuclear program. There are also many examples of illicit Iranian procurements for its nuclear program where Iranian and other trading companies misrepresented the end use to suppliers.

This architecture covering proliferation sensitive goods should remain in place for the duration of the comprehensive agreement. The six powers must carefully plan for eventualities now and design and implement an architecture that prevents future Iranian illicit procurements under a comprehensive agreement.

3) Implement an Additional Protocol "Plus"

Many have discussed conditions necessary to verify an agreement with Iran, particularly ones that would supplement the Additional Protocol, sometimes collectively called the Additional Protocol "Plus" or "AP Plus". Despite its central importance, the Additional Protocol by itself is necessary but not sufficient to verify a comprehensive solution with Iran. These supplementary provisions will need to create a guarantee of snap inspections, sometimes called anywhere, anytime inspections, and a critical baseline of information, including how many centrifuges Iran has made, how much natural uranium it has produced and is producing annually, and its inventory of raw materials and equipment for its centrifuge program. This baseline is necessary if the agreement is to provide assurances about the absence of secret nuclear activities and facilities.

With regard to establishing a baseline on the number of centrifuges made by Iran, verification of centrifuge manufacturing is necessary, including the declaration and verification of key raw materials and components. The declaration needs to include the origin and amounts of key raw materials and the total number of major components, including the number held in stock, the number manufactured or procured, and their fate. A description of the locations used to produce these goods will also be needed.

Another element is the rigorous verification of uranium obtained abroad and produced domestically, such as in uranium mines and mills. The amounts of uranium will need to be carefully verified.

A third step is that Iran would agree to provide the IAEA with details of past and future imports, exports, and uses of key items listed under INFCIRC 254 part 1 and 2 and other critical goods that are used in Iran's nuclear programs.

A fourth area is the verification of any past activities related to the separation of plutonium. These declarations should include information on any actual or attempted procurements related to acquiring capabilities to separate plutonium from irradiated material.

A fifth element is language that guarantees on-going visits and verification of any key facilities, materials, and components associated with the former military dimensions of Iran's nuclear programs. These verification activities would follow Iran's satisfying the IAEA's concerns about the military dimensions of its nuclear programs. These on-going activities would help provide assurance that no undeclared weaponization activities have resumed.

The deal will need to carefully establish more intrusive inspection arrangements than those found in existing safeguards agreements. The IAEA has powerful inspection tools, including special inspections in the comprehensive safeguards agreement and managed access in the Additional Protocol,[6] which can enable inspectors to access undeclared sites and locations. However, in both cases, there is a consultation process, which the IAEA would need to go through with Iran. Although the IAEA has methods to call for an inspection without delay, ultimately, the IAEA depends on the cooperation of the state, and it has to be ready to justify its needs for access. This situation is inadequate in a deal with Iran.

Because of Iran's history of denying or delaying the IAEA access to sites, taking actions to hide activities at sites, and generally abusing the consultation process with the inspectors, a deal needs to include legally binding provisions that ensure the IAEA prompt access to sites. The IAEA

---

[6] Article 4.d of Additional Protocol.

must have the ability to conduct snap inspections, or anytime, anywhere inspections on notice, during the life of an agreement.

Thank you for the opportunity to testify today.

Appendix 1[7]:

Specific Violations of the Comprehensive Safeguards Agreement, Pre-2004

From the mid-1980s to 2003 Iran violated its safeguards agreement with the IAEA by failing to declare numerous activities required by Iran's safeguards agreement with the IAEA, primarily involving experiments with nuclear material. Though several IAEA reports describe these violations, the November 2004 IAEA safeguards report on Iran provides an especially detailed summary of Iran's overall nuclear program, including specific NPT violations.[8] According to the IAEA, Iran failed to declare the following major activities:

• **Uranium Imports:** Iran failed to report that it had purchased natural uranium (1,000 kg of UF6, 400 kg of UF4, and 400 kg of UO2) from China in 1991, and its subsequent transfer for further processing. Iran acknowledged the imports in February 2003.

• **Uranium conversion:** Iran did not inform the IAEA of its use of the imported uranium in tests of its uranium conversion processes, including "uranium dissolution, purification using pulse columns, and the production of uranium metal, and the associated production and loss of nuclear material." Iran acknowledged this failure in February 2003.

• **Uranium enrichment:** Iran failed to report that it had used 1.9 kg of the imported UF6 to test P1 centrifuges at the Kalaye Electric Company centrifuge workshop in 1999 and 2002. In its October 2003 declaration to the IAEA, Iran first admitted to introducing UF6 into a centrifuge in 1999, and into as many as 19 centrifuges in 2002. Iran also failed to declare the associated production of enriched and depleted uranium.

• **Hidden Sites:** Iran did not declare to the IAEA the existence of a pilot enrichment facility at the Kalaye Electric Company Workshop, and laser enrichment plants at the Tehran Nuclear Research center and at Lashkar Ab'ad. Because experiments at these sites involved the use of nuclear material in equipment, Iran was obligated to report them to the IAEA.

• **Laser Isotope Enrichment Experiments:** Iran failed to report that in 1993 it imported 50 kg of natural uranium metal, and that it used 8 kg of this for atomic vapor laser isotope separation (AVLIS) experiments at Tehran Nuclear Research Center from 1999 to 2000, and 22 kg of the metal for AVLIS experiments at Lashkar Ab'ad from 2002 to 2003.[9] These activities were ultimately acknowledged in an October 2003 declaration.

• **Plutonium Experiments:** Iran did not report to the IAEA that it had produced uranium dioxide (UO2) targets, irradiated them in the Tehran Research Reactor, and then separated the plutonium from the irradiated targets. Iran also failed to report the production and transfer of waste associated with these activities and that it had stored unprocessed irradiated targets at the Tehran Nuclear Research Center. In later meetings with the IAEA, Iran said that it conducted the plutonium separation experiments between 1988 and 1993 using shielded glove boxes at the Tehran Nuclear Research Center.

---

[7] Excerpted from Albright and Jacqueline Shire, "Iran's NPT Violations – Numerous and Possibly Ongoing?" ISIS Report, September 29, 2006. http://isis-online.org/uploads/isis-reports/documents/irannptviolations.pdf
[8] http://www.iaea.org/Publications/Documents/Board/2004/gov2004-83.pdf
[9] International Atomic Energy Agency, "Implementation of the NPT Safeguards Agreement in the Islamic Republic of Iran." GOV/2003/75. 10 November 2003, Annex 1. p. 2. 3

Appendix 2:

Major Illicit Iranian Procurements in Violation of UN Security Council Sanctions and National Trade Controls

Iran's wide-ranging illicit procurement efforts have centered on outfitting its gas centrifuge program and Arak nuclear reactor project in defiance of a host of supplier countries' national trade controls and of United Nations Security Council sanctions resolutions that require Iran to suspend both programs.[10] The UN Security Council first passed a resolution demanding a suspension of Iran's nuclear programs in 2006 under resolution 1696.[11] But Iran continued to conduct smuggling operations regularly to outfit its sanctioned nuclear programs. Intelligence agencies and the IAEA found that Iran also conducted illicit procurement to supply its secret nuclear weapons program until at least 2004;[12] European countries have detected procurements after 2004 related to nuclear weapons development.[13] Iran continues these operations throughout the period of the Joint Plan of Action, although the agreement did not explicitly denote that Iran would suspend illicit procurement activities.

Some prominent examples of major procurements made or attempted by Iran in recent years include:

• In 2012, a major U.S. sting operation led to the arrest of an Iranian working with a Chinese company to send or attempt to send U.S. and European-origin goods to Iran and Iranian companies or entities via transshipment through China. The sought-after goods, which included tons of maraging steel, vacuum pumps, pressure transducers, mass spectrometers, and accessories, were dual-use items intended for and critical to the operation and advancement of Iran's gas centrifuge program.[14]

• Qiang Hu, a Chinese citizen, was charged in the United States for violating U.S. export controls by selling thousands of pressure transducers, which measure pressure in gas centrifuge cascades, to unnamed customers through his position of sales manager at MKS Instruments Shanghai Ltd. in China.[15] Iran was a likely recipient. Hu worked with two colleagues and two phony Chinese trading companies to fraudulently obtain U.S. export licenses for over $6.5 million worth of pressure transducers.

---

[10] For additional. detailed examples. see ISIS. "Illicit Trade: Case Studies." http://isis-online.org/studies/category/illicit-trade/

[11] United Nations Security Council Resolution 1696 (2006), July 31, 2006. http://www.isisnucleariran.org/assets/pdf/UNSC_res_1696.pdf

[12] Report by the Director General, *International Atomic Energy Agency (IAEA), Implementation of the NPT Safeguards Agreement and the relevant provisions of Security Council resolutions in the Islamic Republic of Iran*, November 8, 2011. http://isis-online.org/uploads/isis-reports/documents/IAEA_Iran_8Nov2011.pdf

[13] David Albright and Christina Walrond, *The Trials of the German-Iranian Trader Mohsen Vanaki: The German Federal Intelligence Service Assesses that Iran Likely Has a Nuclear Weapons Program*, ISIS Report, December 15, 2009. http://isis-online.org/uploads/isis-reports/documents/MohsenCaseStudy_update_15Dec2009.pdf

[14] David Albright and Andrea Stricker, "Major U.S. Sting Operation Arrests Iranian in Nuclear Smuggling Network," ISIS, August 12, 2012. http://isis-online.org/uploads/isis-reports/documents/US_case_gas_centrifuge_equipment.pdf

[15] Department of Justice Press Release, "Chinese National Charged in Massachusetts with Illegal Exports of Sensitive Technology to China," May 23, 2012. http://www.justice.gov/usao/ma/news/2012/May/HUQiangchargesPR.html.

• A Swedish naturalized citizen, originally from Iran, was convicted in 2013 for running a small Swedish trading company that attempted to illegally export gas centrifuge relevant valves and vacuum pumps to Iran. Many previous dual-use exports to Iran were successful.[16]

• In 2011, an Iranian trading company, Jahan Tech Rooyan Pars Co., sought via a commercial Chinese web site 100,000 ring magnets, whose dimensions matched those of ring magnets of Iran's IR-1 centrifuge. This number of ring magnets was enough for 50,000 IR-1 centrifuges.[17]

• According to a senior U.S. official interviewed by The Washington Post, Iran was detected in 2010 trying to buy carbon fiber in China, a material used in fabricating advanced gas centrifuges.[18]

• In 2009, a Chinese company, Roc-Master Manufacture and Supply Company, working on behalf of an Iranian client, brokered a deal for 108 European-made pressure transducers with a distributor of this equipment located in Taiwan. The Taiwanese distributor misled the European manufacturer that the end user was in China, but instead forwarded the pressure transducers to Iran.[19]

• Starting in 2007 and continuing into 2011, Iran sought 1,767 valves from Germany for its IR-40 heavy water reactor at Arak and planned to pay $6 million for these valves.[20] The Iran-based Modern Industries Technique Company (MITEC) which is responsible for the design and construction of the Arak reactor, was the entity that sought the valves abroad. MITEC has been listed under United Nations Security Council sanctions since 2010. The major players in the procurement scheme, including Hossein Tanideh, an Iranian procurement agent, were arrested in Turkey and Germany.

• From 2006 to the present, the United States has tracked a Chinese company's sales of missile and nuclear related materials to Iran, including illegally accessing the U.S. financial system to receive payments from Iran. The prominent case of the sanctioned Chinese company, Limmt, and its owner, Li Fang-Wei, has showcased China's inaction on enforcing sanctions against Iran.[21] In 2009, the United States first indicted Li and Limmt, and in 2014, the United States released a new indictment and a reward for Li's arrest.[22]

• In 2006, a private Chinese manufacturing company under false pretenses acquired vacuum pump systems from a European company's Chinese subsidiary. These pumps were manufactured in Europe and

[16] Swedish indictment of Shahab Ghasri, September 24, 2011.
http://www.exponerat.info/wpcontent/uploads/2012/12/iranier_Smuggling-tekn-utrust-Iran-B-3487-11-stämning.pdf
; Report of the Panel of Experts on Iran established pursuant to resolution 1929 (2010), June 5, 2013, paras 23-27 and 111.
[17] David Albright, "Ring Magnets for IR-1 Centrifuges," ISIS Report, February 13, 2013. http://isis-online.org/uploads/isis-reports/documents/iran_ring_magnet_13Feb2013.pdf
[18] John Pomfret, "Chinese Firms Bypass Sanctions on Iran, U.S. Says," The Washington Post, October 18, 2010.
[19] "How Nuclear Equipment Reached Iran," The Associated Press. March 1, 2010.
[20] Cathrin Gilbert, Holger Stark, and Andreas Ulrich, "Operation Ventilator," Der Speigel, 40/2012. See also Report of the Panel of Experts on Iran, June 5, 2013.
[21] Andrea Stricker, "A Smuggler's Use of the U.S. Financial System to Receive Illegal Payments from Iran," ISIS Report, October 23, 2009, updated February 11, 2011. http://isis-online.org/uploads/isisreports/documents/Limmt_Li_Fang_Wei_23Oct2009_update9Feb2011.pdf
[22] David Albright, Andrea Stricker, and Donald Stewart, "Serial Proliferator Karl Li: China's Continued Refusal to Act," ISIS Report, May 8, 2014. http://isis-online.org/isis-reports/detail/serial-proliferator-karl-li-chinas-continued-refusal-to-act/20

intended for use exclusively in China. Nonetheless, the Chinese manufacturing company sent them to Iran without official approval.[23]

• In the last few years, Iran acquired significant quantities of high quality carbon fiber, a good usable in its advanced gas centrifuges. The carbon fiber, made in Japan, was sold to a U.S. company, which in turn sold it to an EU country. It was subsequently sold to other companies within the EU, and ultimately trucked to Iran via Turkey.

---

[23] David Albright, Paul Brannan, and Andrea Scheel, "How Cooperation between a Company and Government Authorities Disrupted a Sophisticated Illicit Iranian Procurement," ISIS Report, January 12, 2009. http://isisonline.org/uploads/isis-reports/documents/Pumps_China_12January2009.pdf

Appendix 3:

Update on the IAEA/Iran Framework for Cooperation and Resolution of Possible Military Dimensions (PMD): Effort Remains Stalled

Iran has pledged under a Framework for Cooperation with the IAEA to resolve all outstanding issues relating to the possible military dimensions of its nuclear program. These issues were detailed in an annex in the IAEA's November 2011 safeguards report.[24] The evidence underlying the outstanding issues is viewed by the IAEA as "overall, credible." Iran has told the IAEA that "'most of the issues' in the Annex to GOV/2011/65 (the November 2011 safeguards report) were 'mere allegations and do not merit consideration.'"[25]

The IAEA reiterated in September 2014 that with regard to its investigation:

> *The Board of Governors has confirmed on numerous occasions, since as early as 1992, that para. 2 of INFCIRC/153 (Corr.), which corresponds to Article 2 of Iran's Safeguards Agreement, authorizes and requires the Agency to seek to verify both the non-diversion of nuclear material from declared activities (i.e. correctness) and the absence of undeclared nuclear activities in the State (i.e. completeness).*

The IAEA has stated it needs to conduct a "system" assessment of the outstanding PMD issues, and that "this will involve considering and acquiring an understanding of each issue in turn, and then integrating all of the issues into a "system" and assessing that system as a whole."

Although Iran has pledged to cooperate on addressing the past and present issues related to the possible military dimensions of its nuclear program, the latest IAEA Iran safeguards report from February 19, 2015 notes no further progress on resolving them. In particular, Iran has not proposed any new practical measures to resolve its PMD file in a fourth step under the IAEA/Iran Framework for Cooperation. It has also not addressed the last two measures in the third step of the Framework for Cooperation that had been agreed upon in May 2014. These two measures concern the initiation of high explosives and neutron transport calculations possibly related to the development of nuclear weapons. In August 2014, the IAEA had also invited Iran to propose new measures for a new step in the Framework for Cooperation, but, as of early March 2015, Iran has failed to do so.

Requests to Access Parchin Site

In February 2012 the IAEA requested a visit to a site at the Parchin military site which it has not yet been granted. Instead, the IAEA (and ISIS) has tracked via satellite imagery the apparent sanitization efforts by Iran to conceal past activities at the site over the past two plus years since the IAEA first asked to visit.[26] The IAEA reports that the activities that have taken place at the site since its request for access have likely "undermined its ability to conduct effective verification" and that Iran must address its questions and provide access to the site.

---

[24] Report by the Director General, *Implementation of the NPT Safeguards Agreement and relevant provisions of Security Council Resolutions in the Islamic Republic of Iran*, GOV/2011/65, November 8, 2011. http://isis-online.org/uploads/isis-reports/documents/IAEA_Iran_8Nov2011.pdf

[25] Report by the Director General, *Implementation of the NPT Safeguards Agreement and relevant provisions of Security Council Resolutions in the Islamic Republic of Iran*, GOV/2014/43, September 5, 2014. http://isis-online.org/uploads/isis-reports/documents/gov-2014-43.pdf

[26] "Iran: ISIS Reports with Imagery." http://isis-online.org/isis-reports/imagery/category/iran/

The IAEA reported in its February 2015 safeguards report viewing in satellite imagery further activity at the Parchin military site. It has observed construction materials, vehicles, and other equipment present at a specific location at Parchin where the nuclear weapons-related high explosive activities are alleged to have taken place. Similarly, through analysis of commercial satellite imagery dated between August 12, 2014 and January 31, 2015, ISIS also detected various activities and the presence of construction materials at the site in question. In the most recent imagery, resurfacing or re-asphalting activities could be seen as well as cleanup of construction materials and debris, all of which would be consistent with the IAEA's findings.[27]

---

[27] David Albright, Serena Kelleher-Vergantini, and Christopher Coughlin, "Modifications at the Parchin Site: A Comprehensive Timeline; New Imagery Suggests Re-Asphalting," ISIS Report, February 11, 2015. http://isis-online.org/uploads/isis-reports/documents/Parchin_February_11_2015_Final.pdf

Ms. Ros-Lehtinen. Thank you very much. Excellent panelists and I would like to ask unanimous consent that our subcommittee recognize our special guest who is with us, Mr. Trent Franks, for a statement he would like to make.

Mr. Franks. Thank you kindly, Madam Chair. I appreciate your holding this hearing so very much and as it happens Ms. Heinrichs was the military legislative assistant in our office and she taught us essentially everything we know about missile defense. And we are just extremely proud of the direction that she has gone, that she is able to teach other Members of Congress and I think she is a force that is important to the world and I really appreciate you being able to hear her testimony today. I don't want to embarrass her. She didn't know I was doing this, but we are very impressed with all the great things she is doing. And with that, I am just grateful for the opportunity and I yield back.

Ms. Ros-Lehtinen. Well, thank you so much and I think that that was an accurate assessment of her capabilities and she made a most excellent presentation. So trained by the best. I don't know which way that training went. I think knowing you, Trent, it went toward you. But thank you so much and I am so pleased with the testimony today and with the members present and this is an extremely important topic.

The administration's argument is that this deal will allow us to have the mechanisms in place to monitor and verify Iran's compliance with any final agreement, to hold Iran accountable, and to prevent it from getting a bomb, a wonderful desire, wonderful outcomes. But as most folks pointed out, every indication from past history suggests otherwise, that Iran's continued stonewalling of the IAEA will continue and even during the implementation of the JPOA this stalling and this stonewalling was taking place. So it gives us further cause to be less than optimistic.

As the ranking member pointed out earlier this week, Olli Heinonen, the former Deputy Director General of the IAEA who we have had testify before us and Ray Takeyh, and former NSA and CIA Director General Michael Hayden, stated in an op ed in the Washington Post that even if the nuclear deal manages to push Iran's nuclear breakout time to 1 year, that is the stated goal, this might not be sufficient to detect and reverse the Iranian violations.

So I wanted to ask the panelists what are the difficulties in achieving a verification regime that would be capable of detecting, of testing, of acting to stop Iran from possible breakout for both the IAEA and their standards and the U.S. Intelligence Community? What difficulties do we have in getting such a structure in place?

We will begin with Mr. Tobey.

Mr. Tobey. Thank you, Madam Chair. The difficulties are considerable and they are made worse by what at least has been reported about the shape of the deal. You referenced creating a 1-year breakout time. That, of course, deals only with declared sites. So that would ensure or would aim to ensure that the declared sites were not used to make nuclear weapons. But the problem is that I think most analysts believe that were Iran to move in the direction of nuclear weapons, they would use undeclared sites, covert sites. And the burdens that are placed on any verification program for detecting covert sites are made much more difficult by the allowance of some enrichment work. I know that that has been bitterly disputed as to whether or not Iran should or should not be allowed to have any enrichment capability. But I think it is indisputable that if they have some capability it would be more difficult to verify that that capability isn't being diverted to covert sites.

So that is why it is so centrally important to get to the bottom of the so-called possible military dimensions that all of you have referenced, all of us have referenced. All of us in this room understand the importance of that issue. And I think it has to be gotten to the bottom of in order to ensure that future activity——

Ms. Ros-Lehtinen. Absolutely.

Mr. Tobey. It is not about the past. It is about the future.

Ms. Ros-Lehtinen. Absolutely. Ms. Heinrichs?

Ms. Heinrichs. I agree with what my colleague just said. I will also just like to point out that because the nuclear program is so inextricably tied to their missile program, the missile component is something that hasn't been discussed as what it should be. But missile detection is much easier to do than to detect the weaponization elements of the nuclear program.

And so we can already see what they are doing with their missile program. So Mr. Tobey is correct. It is almost impossible to get to the bottom of the verification if they don't even disclose what they have done in the past. And we need to do that first. But I would suggest that an easier, possibly an easier way to actually see what they are doing is just look to see their massive missile program.

Ms. Ros-Lehtinen. Very good point. Mr. Albright?

Mr. Albright. The administration's goal of having a 1-year breakout criteria makes sense. I mean you need something to drive in negotiations.

As Mr. Tobey pointed out and it is easier to apply to declared facilities and where the difficulty is, of course, is if Iran is going to try to do covertly. And I would say may do a hybrid or using declared and undeclared facilities. So there are many paths to the bomb.

But I think the verification, if done rigorously, can actually lead to a situation where you could do this in a year. But it certainly would, from my point of view would need to include coming clean on PMD. You would have to be able to make sure Iran isn't smuggling goods in for a covert site, so you would need the U.N. Security Council sanctions to remain in place for the duration of the deal. If it has to empower or give more tools to the inspectors, they are going to have to be able to go, in a sense, very quick notice to sites where there are suspicions. They are going to have to have access. And so you are going to have to wire all this in an agreement. And if it isn't wired in an agreement, then I think it will be very hard to satisfy the 1-year criteria for undeclared sites.

Ms. Ros-Lehtinen. True. Now as we know, Iran impedes any and all IAEA inspections that it can that may be related in any way to its suspect activities including the PMD. And we were talking about the snap inspections, the any time, anywhere inspections. Many people believe that we need that in order for this deal to be credible.

How likely is it that the Iran deal will include these inspection parameters that they will have this snap, any time, anywhere inspections? Will we insist on it? Will the IAEA insist on it? The Intelligence Community, will they be satisfied with what is in the deal to detect Iran's noncompliance if these snap inspections were not guaranteed in any final agreement?

Mr. TOBEY. With respect to the any time, anywhere inspections, I don't know whether or not those will be a part of the agreement. But I would point out that there are other elements that may be as or more important. It is an important deterrent to have the ability for inspectors to go any place any time. But it is not how you generally detect a covert operation or a covert nuclear capability. That is done by talking to people, by examining records, by much broader declarations as Mr. Albright already referenced, by the sort of patient and careful work that would lead inspectors to understand that covert activity is underway. And it is only at the last moment that one would actually take the final step to go and visit a site.

Ms. ROS-LEHTINEN. They have to do their homework before to be able to have that snap inspection.

Mr. TOBEY. Absolutely. So all of that work is at least as important as the ability to go any time any where.

Ms. ROS-LEHTINEN. Thank you. I believe the only real way to prevent Iran's breakout is to dismantle its nuclear infrastructure. As long as we are only getting access to what Iran wants us to see, there is no way to know, as you pointed out, the real extent of Iran's nuclear program. And the current JPOA is limited to only declared sites, as you pointed out. It is the undeclared sites that should really worry us.

Mr. Tobey, you stated that by doing this it actually facilitates Iran's ability to cheat. If you could explain that.

Mr. TOBEY. I am sorry, by doing——

Ms. ROS-LEHTINEN. The current JPOA is limited to only declared nuclear facilities and by doing this, we are actually perpetuating that

Mr. TOBEY. Exactly. The focus of the talks has been creating this 1 year breakout time. So we have gone from a situation where the President's originally-stated goal was preventing Iran from getting a nuclear weapon. In other words, changing their strategic calculus. Now our goal is putting a 1-year speed bump between Iran and a nuclear weapon. Unfortunately, that applies only to declared sites. And the only way to get at undeclared sites is a two-fold operation which Mr. Albright has already referenced. One is to get to the bottom of these so-called possible military dimensions and the second is to be able to understand and monitor all of the equipment and materials that Iran is either importing or creating itself that would be applicable to making nuclear weapons. So without those two elements any agreement would not be verifiable.

Ms. ROS-LEHTINEN. And Mr. Albright, getting back to the snap inspections that you were talking about, how can the IAEA monitor and verify any Iranian activity at sites that are actually undeclared? If you could push that button.

Mr. ALBRIGHT. You asked would this be an agreement. I mean I think there is worry that it won't be. There is certainly indications that the administration is making compromises and the Iranians have been very tough on this. This was told to me by one of

42

the negotiators well over a year ago that the Revolutionary Guard had sent a signal through the Iranian negotiators that there was no way the IAEA would be allowed to visit military or Revolutionary Guard sites. And so that was stated as one of the essentially two major redlines. And of course, that is unacceptable, but will the U.S. push hard enough to overcome this redline and get to an ability to have anywhere any time inspections.

Now of course, we will see, but I do worry about it and I think that without those I would expect they wouldn't get the broader declarations too, that there is a real risk that you won't have the package of measures needed to do adequate verification.

Ms. ROS-LEHTINEN. It would be interesting to see. And one last question and I thank the members for allowing me all this time and you will have that time as well.

Ms. Heinrichs, you have done extensive work on Iran's ballistic missile program and as you pointed out in your testimony, written and verbal, several U.N. Security Council resolutions explicitly seek to curb Iran's missile program. But how closely related are Iran's progress on its ballistic missile program and its nuclear program? And do you think that the negotiations will include or should have included other aspects of Iran's dangerous activities including its support for terror, its ballistic missile program?

We had a full committee hearing last week and I think Mr. Blinken, we asked him is Iran the foremost state sponsor of terrorism and he said it is among the top. I can't even imagine except for North Korea who is in that league. But if you could tell us about the ballistic missile program and other aspects of Iran's dangerous behavior?

Ms. HEINRICHS. Thank you for the question. I think it is possibly one of the most important questions. Iran's nuclear program is inextricably tied to its ballistic missile program. They go hand in glove. So if we simply pause their enrichment capability, for instance, they have already mastered the ability to enrich, and they are very patient, so they can go ahead and take a pause on that. And then continue the more difficult aspects of their program which is their delivery system, their ballistic missile system.

So ballistic missiles, they are relatively cheap, if you are going to try to pose an asymmetric threat to a country that is much more militarily sophisticated than Iran, like the United States. And that is exactly what the Iranians have been working on doing. They have just successfully orbited their fourth satellite which is that technology is directly transferrable to an ICBM capability and the Intelligence Community still assesses that Iran will be able to test an ICBM capability which would give them an ability to coerce the United States' homeland by this year.

Ms. ROS-LEHTINEN. Mr. Deutch is recognized.

Mr. DEUTCH. Thanks, Madam Chairman. Mr. Albright, during these negotiations we have been told that the goal ultimately is to cut off the four pathways to a nuclear bomb for Iran: Fordow, Natanz, Arak, and covert program. Are those the only four?

Mr. ALBRIGHT. That covers it. I think there is always more, but that is the main pathways that the administration needs to worry about.

Mr. DEUTCH. And the access, the unprecedented access that we are told we received during this JPOA, during the interim deal, does not include any where, any time inspections?

Mr. ALBRIGHT. No.

Mr. DEUTCH. What do we have now?

Mr. ALBRIGHT. Well, there is better monitoring at declared sites and there is some more openness at parts of the centrifuge manufacturing complex. But in general, no. The measures that were put forth as part of the JPOA were never intended to be able to increase the IAEA's ability to detect covert sites.

Mr. DEUTCH. So what is it going forward? You said we need any where any time inspections and that those need to be in place for at least 20 years. Is that, given the reports in the news, would that be 10 years beyond the deal or would that be—would that require a deal that is 20 years long?

Mr. ALBRIGHT. It could be done independently of the limits on the nuclear program. I mean one would assume that when it is on the Arak reactor are indefinite. They won't be reversible, so once they are put in place there will just be limits on the ability to make weapon-grade plutonium.

On the centrifuge number, those could be lifted after some period of time. These inspection arrangements, these broader verification requirements must continue past that, I would argue. You are going to need them for a long time. In a sense, Iran has been in noncompliance for 20 years. I mean it has severe lack of credibility and 10 years is just not enough.

Mr. DEUTCH. What does that mean, they have been in noncompliance? Take a step back. We are all steeped in this. We have been focused on this for a long time. For people who are tuning in to these talks because it is the very end and there is a lot of talk to understand about striking a deal with Iran and stopping it from acquiring nuclear weapons. Why are we concerned? What have they done wrong all this period? And weaponization and creation of a bomb, but they tell us they want to have a peaceful nuclear program. For people who haven't paid attention, explain to them why this matters so much.

Mr. ALBRIGHT. It is a little bit like someone who breaks the law. Iran has been deceiving the IAEA, the international community, for 20 years or so. And its intention was to put together in secret nuclear capabilities and part of that capability appears to have been oriented to getting nuclear weapons. So in a sense you have a situation where they have been caught and convicted. That is in the sense what the U.N. Security Council resolutions signify and that they are on probation. And we need time in order to verify that they are reformed. And in that period you need to limit their ability, in a sense their freedoms to move on nuclear programs.

Mr. DEUTCH. And they have not verified anything to date. A lot of believe we shouldn't, we can't make a deal, shouldn't consider making a deal if they are not willing to come clean on the past military dimensions of the program. Would it make sense for us to do that?

Mr. ALBRIGHT. Obviously, the administration is thinking about not doing that. I think that is pretty clear. Or doing it in a much more limited way than maybe we have discussed today.

Now I think one of the problems of doing that is if I can go back to the days of the agreed framework, people were really scared of war with North Korea in '94. And a decision was made to call off the inspectors and a deal was made that essentially hobbled the inspectors. They were brought forth to do monitoring and I at the time supported the agreed framework, but I understood its weakness.

In this case, there is a risk that if you don't get the IAEA's strengthened, it doesn't go into this deal knowing what Iran has done in the past, you are hobbling them and undermining their ability to verify. But in this case, unlike the North Korean case, the IAEA is going to be called upon to be the lead investigator in a sense to determine whether Iran is complying.

Mr. DEUTCH. Right, so that is what I want to understand. So the IAEA—Iran has completely stonewalled. They have not been forthcoming. They have not granted the access to the IAEA. They have not answered the questions posed by the IAEA which stem from the fact that we know that as you point out, we know what Iran was trying to do to develop nuclear weapons. They were caught. They were convicted, but we are now at the point where they are not complying with what the world has expected them to comply with, right?

Mr. ALBRIGHT. That is right.

Mr. DEUTCH. So the question is going into a deal, if there is one, regardless of what the deal looks like, if it is the IAEA that is ultimately the entity that is going to monitor and verify whether the terms of a deal are being lived up to by the Iranians, how, number one, how can that happen? How do we trust that that can work given 20 years of experience that we have had with Iran's interaction with the IAEA?

Mr. ALBRIGHT. I would agree that it can't work. I mean it is really—I mean no one is looking for Iran to have a mea culpa. It would be nice and it would be very helpful, but there are ways to do this sort of thing. But Iran can't continue to—it essentially almost abused the IAEA. They issue reports. One came out a couple of weeks ago which just belittles the IAEA. And also in that report, they argue strongly that the IAEA's verification as it exists today should be weakened. So you have a situation that is unacceptable and Iran does need to face up and make changes in how it views verification and how it treats the IAEA and how it satisfies the IAEA's condition.

And I would say that it may be that in the way the administration is negotiating this is that you can't force Iran to do this before the deal is signed, but you certainly can say no sanctions relief until they at least make concrete progress on addressing the IAEA's concerns.

Mr. DEUTCH. Right. So the question is if you—if there is a deal that is reached, the moment that a deal is struck if there is sanctions relief of any kind and according to the reports in the press which is what we have to go by on the current negotiations, according to the reports in the press, Iran's sticking point is that they want massive sanctions relief or total sanctions relief at the outset. If you provide any sort of significant sanctions relief the day the agreement is signed, you will have rewarded Iran for 20 years of bad behavior, flouting international norms, and ignoring the demands of the IAEA. Isn't that right?

Mr. ALBRIGHT. Yes, I agree.

Mr. DEUTCH. And finally, if the goal is a year's breakout time and we have just gone through all these concerns about the IAEA, is a year enough time? Is that goal enough for the IAEA to detect a potential breakout, to verify it, and then take action to stop it, particularly given that there are other countries Iran may argue the other countries, the P5+1, the U.N. may be brought in, is a year breakout time realistic if the IAEA is the entity that is tasked with enforcing it?

Mr. ALBRIGHT. At declared sites, I think it is. And again, I think some of this depends on the U.S. being willing to take military action if it believes there has been a violation and it is confirmed. And the idea with the year is that there would be enough time to gather international support to avoid that. But in the end, some of this is going to rest on the U.S. being willing to do that.

Now in the covert sites, if the verification is not improved from what would be traditional IAEA safeguards and additional protocol, then it is going to be tough. I mean you could easily have had a situation with Iran where you do spend a year arguing in the United States, internationally, on what has happened, is it really a violation? You may have trouble pulling together a coalition and the U.S. may be put in a position of having to decide does it take military action when there is deep opposition to that military action? But if the verification arrangements are done properly, then I think a year can be enough. But it is going to require a very intrusive verification system and it is unclear if that can be accomplished.

Mr. DEUTCH. Madam Chairman, I appreciate the indulgence. Anything short of that then, anything short of unprecedented any where any time inspections demanded by the world of Iran which Iran should comply with given their history and given what else would be included in this deal, anything short of that makes that 1-year breakout time which has been the goal we have been told of these entire negotiations significantly perhaps dramatically less than 1 year leaving us with a dramatically reduced period of time in which to respond.

Mr. ALBRIGHT. Could be, but the one thing I would say any where any time is not unprecedented. That language is adopted from what South Africa said it would do after it decided to come clean about its past nuclear weapons program which also was a big fight. South Africa refused to do that initially despite the evidence, but under pressure decided to come clean and accepted this idea of anywhere any time inspection. So I think it is not unprecedented. But I do think that there is a lot of parts to verification. And so I wouldn't want to say that if you don't get one exactly as you need it, that the thing falls apart. You have to look at it system wide. But without any time any where inspections, the job gets much harder.

Mr. DEUTCH. I appreciate that, Madam Chairman, thank you and I thank the other witnesses for your testimony. I didn't want to exclude you, but I am out of time. Thank you.

Ms. ROS-LEHTINEN. Thank you very much, Mr. Deutch. Mr. DeSantis of Florida.

Mr. DESANTIS. Mr. Tobey, are you comfortable with the enrichment ability that is contemplated under this deal? It had always been that they were not going to be able to enrich. Now they have a substantial number of centrifuges. Are you comfortable with that?

Mr. TOBEY. The original idea to ban all enrichment was to keep Iran from gaining the technical capacity to understand that, so they couldn't mount a covert effort. Unfortunately, that horse is out of the barn. So the original rationale for that, I think, is diminished. At the same time, zero is a lot easier to verify than some higher number which would allow the technology and equipment perhaps to be diverted.

So while I think it is not an ideal situation, the only terms under which I would be comfortable is if we had two additional verification provisions. One would be to get to the bottom of the possible military dimensions as we have talked about and the second would be to have firm control over the materials and equipment that Iran either produces or imports as Mr. Albright has described. So this would be an ongoing monitoring situation.

And so by allowing some level of enrichment, I think it demands a much more rigorous verification system.

Mr. DESANTIS. The 10-year sunset that is reported, is that adequate?

Mr. TOBEY. It doesn't strike me as adequate. This issue was reported by the IAEA Board of Governors to the U.N. Security Council 10 years ago. I am dumbfounded that we might have an agreement that would be shorter than the time it has taken to negotiate it.

Mr. DESANTIS. Ms. Heinrichs, do you agree with that? Ten years to just simply walk away after 10 years and trust that they are going to behave. Does that bother you?

Ms. HEINRICHS. No, I don't think that we should trust them now. I think 10 years is not adequate because what we really want is for them to make the political decision to move away from a nuclear weapons capability and they have not done that.

Mr. DESANTIS. In terms of the military sites, because it seems to me that if you are not having any type of inspection of those sites, if there are secret sites, we have no reason to take Iran at its word, it seems to me that they could abide by the deal in the sense of allowing full inspections and yet they could still end up developing a nuclear weapon, correct?

Mr. TOBEY. One thing that I would point out is that Secretary Kerry, I think reasonably, said it is unacceptable for Iran to be 2 months away, to have a 2-month breakout. If it is unacceptable today, I don't understand why it becomes any more acceptable 10 or 15 years from now and at least what has been reported was that the broad restrictions in the Iranian program would fall away after 10 or 15 years which would enable them to move right back to that 2-month breakout period.

Mr. DESANTIS. Even if the inspections were allowed to go to these sites, if the military sites are not included, then they could conceivably keep the deal with respect to those inspections, but still develop a capacity. Is that inaccurate?

Mr. ALBRIGHT. It is a fear. I mean if the IAEA can't do its job and get to the bottom of what has happened, the PMD issues, namely, and then be able to continue verifying no activity at those sites and among those people and potentially other sites, then it would be an agreement where Iran could just wait it out.

But the idea is that you try to at least have restrictions on the program for a generation. That was the goal. Looking back a year, the goal was to have restrictions, pretty strict restrictions on the whole program for a year, intrusive verification, and then over that period of time you would then develop confidence that they wouldn't try to get weapons in the future.

Mr. DESANTIS. Or give time to have a change in the regime or change in the nature of the regime.

Mr. ALBRIGHT. That is right. And so if you shorten that, and it is just 10 years, then of course, you have to worry more. Now I would say be careful. We don't know the details. The administration is going out of its way to confuse us, I will admit, when they talk about using double digits or they use terms like at least 10 years. They talk about phasing on the enrichment programs. So I think the situation is very confused. But I do think it is very logical to demand that the verification conditions either be permanent or last at least a generation. And I think that has be a very clear message that the administration hears.

Mr. DESANTIS. Look, I am mindful about kind of jumping on some of these reports. At the same time, you do look at the behavior of the Gulf States and what they see. Their behavior is not very comforting in terms of this being a deal that they have confidence in, and obviously they fear an Iranian bomb very much.

Look, my bottom line is we have seen different examples of this where North Korea, obviously, didn't work. I think Gaddafi feared he was going to be removed from power. He really was worried about the threat of military force. And I just wonder whether Iran really believes that that credible threat is on the table. And if they don't, then man, I think that they have every incentive to want to cheat this deal. I am over my time and I will yield back. I am good. Thank you.

Ms. ROS-LEHTINEN. Thank you very much, Mr. DeSantis. And thank you, Mr. Boyle, from Pennsylvania. Thank you, sir.

Mr. BOYLE. As you might remember from my brief opening remarks, consistent with what I think pretty much everyone who has spoken on both sides of the aisle here, I come to this whole issue as someone who is highly skeptical that we could reach an agreement that reasonable people would have full confidence in.

That said, it is worth remembering, I think it was Ms. Heinrichs who quoted President Reagan, ''Trust, but verify.'' He quoted the Russian proverb, ''Doverai no proveryai.'' The reason why we remember that is because it was said at a signing ceremony with Mikhail Gorbachev. And so those agreements that after the failure at Reykjavik, when the agreements were signed in '87 and '88, they were criticized at the time by some as naive and going too far. And I would say that history proved them—proved President Reagan pretty well in terms of reaching those agreements.

48

So toward that end, while I am highly skeptical given Iran's repeated history of bad faith behavior with the IAEA and with the international community and being with one of the largest, if not the largest, exporters of terror in the world, all of that having been said, if by some grace of God a new leadership were to come in Tehran, actual, real, Western-oriented, moderate, who wanted Iran to rejoin the international world, and give up this path that they have been on over the last three and a half decades, what would a real agreement look like that each of you would say that is something that is worth signing? That is something that we could place trust in and actually have real confidence that it was actually an agreement worth signing?

Mr. TOBEY. In terms of a technical model, it has already been referenced, the South Africa example is probably a good one. I would also look for markers of a strategic decision just as you described, that Iran had decided to forego pursuing nuclear weapons in favor of a better relationship with other nations.

Frankly, I do come back again to this possible military dimensions issue. If they are not willing to come clean on that, it not only makes verification more difficult, but it is a marker of Iranian intent because they clearly want to hide something in order to preserve it.

And so I would say that an agreement that looked like it was going to be useful and that is what I think all of us here seek. I mean the reason we have criticisms about what may be taking place is because we want a better deal, not because we don't want a deal. It would be to get to the bottom of that issue.

Ms. HEINRICHS. I appreciate the question. I would agree that we have to get to the bottom of the possible military dimensions, but again, I think it is a bit of a litmus test to look at their missile program. There is no reason that the Iranians need to be as dedicated to their massive ballistic missile arsenal that they have if they don't intend to use it for coercion. And who are they trying to coerce? It is the United States. It is the United States' influence in the region. And so I think unless we see a political decision or a strategic decision of the Iranians to move away from this ballistic missile capability, which I believe is inextricably tied to their nuclear program, and then allow complete unfettered access of the IAEA to its nuclear program to show that they are actually coming clean, essentially, the South Africa example being a good one, then we should not trust them enough to secure a diplomatic solution to this problem.

Mr. ALBRIGHT. I think one of the worries that was alluded to earlier that they will just wait it out. They did some of that during the time of the suspension from '03 to '06 and President Rouhani bragged about how they were able to advance while waiting it out. So I think one of the concerns now is that the pattern of the Iranians appears to be to basically say that yes, we will give up the IR1s which are pretty decrepit machines, but we want to be able to advance our centrifuges and build advanced ones and keep that program alive.

And I think that this deal is going to be much less worthwhile if Iran succeeds in being able to do centrifuge R&D on a substantial basis and I think there is a real worry that that could happen.

And clearly, it is where I think the Iranians are building their narrative. And the U.S. has invested a lot into capping and reducing the IR1 program which may be the thing that Rouhani cares least about at this point in time. Certainly, the nuclear people probably don't care about.

Some other things that are very important is and I think the administration has made progress is in getting rid of the stocks of well-enriched uranium in Iran. They can't stay there. Whether they are in hexafluoride form or oxide, they should leave the country. So I think they have made good progress on getting that established, but whether Iran will go along or not is still an open question, but if there are very minimal stocks in Iran, then that would be—that would build confidence in this deal.

Another thing is that Fordow would be shut down and not involved in any enrichment, that Iran should not have deeply buried sites that contain any gas centrifusion enrichment capability. That is critical, too. Again, I am not sure the administration is going to get that or is even seeking that at this point in time.

So I think that there are many ways you could put together an agreement and I think the administration has thought through all of them and so now the question will be are they going to come up with an agreement with enough of those in there that one can have confidence in.

Mr. BOYLE. Well, I thank you, all three of you and I see I have hit my time limit. But I would just ask in closing and maybe a quick response, South Africa has been referenced a number of times. I think though not on the nuclear part, but in terms of a country that was clearly engaging in terrorism and then actually decided they wanted to rejoin the international world and that was more important to them under the end of Muammar Gaddafi. That is actually an example of a country that remarkably changed its behavior.

I was wondering if we know of any others that we can point to as a potential model to hope and work toward Iran joining?

Mr. BOYLE. There has been other victories, less well known, but Taiwan had a nuclear weapons program and the U.S. intervened politically to end it. And it was done very quietly. So I think there are other victories. Same in South Korea. It was a little tougher there, but—so I think there is ways to do this, but again, I think it depends on the U.S. exerting its influence and the country changing its attitude toward some of these issues.

Mr. Tobey raised this issue of——

Mr. BOYLE. And every one of the examples cited it was ultimately initiated by a decision made in that capital to completely change and which direction it was going and change its priorities and then behavior changes followed that.

Mr. ALBRIGHT. But under a lot of pressure. Those cases involved tremendous amounts of pressure, even South Africa. There were cases, I was told, meetings with nuclear officials in South Africa with U.S. officials where a South African official was fist pounding essentially on the table denying they had a nuclear weapons program just a week or two before de Klerk admitted, yes, we did have one. So I think that pressure matters. And in South Africa, congressional pressure mattered. If you look back in history, you will see that the U.S. Congress played a very important role.

Ms. HEINRICHS. I would just add that it was under enormous political pressure, but it was also in the case of Libya and then as the Intelligence Community has said that they believe that some of the weaponization activities did cease around the 2003 time line, about the time that Libya then voluntarily gave up their WMD program, but it was under the fear of a credible threat of military invasion. It was when the United States went into Iraq. So I think that that is important to keep in mind that without the credible threat of force, that some of these things might not have happened.

Mr. BOYLE. Thank you, Madam Chair.

Ms. ROS-LEHTINEN. Thank you very much and unfortunately that credible show of force is lacking in Iran. The negotiations look to be we are playing a very weak hand and I don't think that pressure is being applied to Iran and Congress has been muted and the sanctions are being lifted and we are in pretty bad shape. But you were wonderful panelists so we thank you very much for being here with us. And with that, the subcommittee is adjourned. Thank you.

[Whereupon, at 3:48 p.m., the subcommittee was adjourned.]

APPENDIX

MATERIAL SUBMITTED FOR THE RECORD

52

SUBCOMMITTEE HEARING NOTICE
COMMITTEE ON FOREIGN AFFAIRS
U.S. HOUSE OF REPRESENTATIVES
WASHINGTON, DC 20515-6128

Subcommittee on the Middle East and North Africa
Ileana Ros-Lehtinen (R-FL), Chairman

March 13, 2015

TO: MEMBERS OF THE COMMITTEE ON FOREIGN AFFAIRS

You are respectfully requested to attend an OPEN hearing of the Committee on Foreign Affairs, to be held by the Subcommittee on the Middle East and North Africa in Room 2172 of the Rayburn House Office Building (and available live on the Committee website at http://www.ForeignAffairs.house.gov):

DATE: Tuesday, March 24, 2015

TIME: 2:00 p.m.

SUBJECT: Iran's Noncompliance with Its International Atomic Energy Agency Obligations

WITNESSES: Mr. William H. Tobey
Senior Fellow
Belfer Center for Science and International Affairs
John F. Kennedy School of Government
Harvard University

Ms. Rebeccah L. Heinrichs
Fellow
George C. Marshall Institute

Mr. David Albright
Founder and President
Institute for Science and International Security

By Direction of the Chairman

COMMITTEE ON FOREIGN AFFAIRS

MINUTES OF SUBCOMMITTEE ON _Middle East and North Africa and Africa, Global Human Rights, and International Organizations_ HEARING

Day __Tuesday__ Date ___3/24/15___ Room ___2172___

Starting Time __2:00 p.m.__ Ending Time __3:48 p.m.__

Recesses [__0__] (____ to ____)(____ to ____)(____ to ____)(____ to ____)(____ to ____)(____ to ____)

Presiding Member(s)

Chairman Ros-Lehtinen

Check all of the following that apply:

Open Session [✓]   Electronically Recorded (taped) [✓]
Executive (closed) Session [✓]   Stenographic Record [✓]
Televised [✓]

TITLE OF HEARING:

Iran's Noncompliance with Its International Atomic Energy Agency Obligations

SUBCOMMITTEE MEMBERS PRESENT:

Chairman Ros-Lehtinen, Reps. Boyle, Clawson, Connolly, DeSantis, Deutch, Frankel and Issa.

NON-SUBCOMMITTEE MEMBERS PRESENT: _(Mark with an * if they are not members of full committee.)_

Rep. Franks

HEARING WITNESSES: Same as meeting notice attached? Yes [✓] No [ ]
(If "no", please list below and include title, agency, department, or organization.)

STATEMENTS FOR THE RECORD: _(List any statements submitted for the record.)_

SFR - Rep. Connolly
Testimony - Dr. Michael Rubin

TIME SCHEDULED TO RECONVENE _____
or
TIME ADJOURNED __3:48 p.m.__

Subcommittee Staff Director

American Enterprise Institute
for Public Policy Research

Statement before the House Committee on Foreign Affairs

Subcommittee on the Middle East and North Africa

"Iran's Noncompliance with its International Atomic Energy Agency Obligations"

Michael Rubin, Ph.D.
Resident Scholar
American Enterprise Institute

March 5, 2015

Madam Chairman, Honorable Members. Thank you for the opportunity to testify on an issue so important to U.S. national security.

Overshadowing this hearing is the Obama administration's diplomacy with Iran and its desire, as Secretary of State John Kerry recently voiced, to have "the benefit of doubt" as the State Department nears its self-imposed deadline to reach a nuclear deal. Concerns loom, however, because as the outlines of a potential agreement take shape, it is clear that the proposals discussed by American and Iranian diplomats fail to resolve basic concerns with regard to Iranian non-compliance with its International Atomic Energy Agency (IAEA) obligations.

Why Iran Can't Be Given "Benefit of the Doubt"
The root of international suspicion with regard to Iran's nuclear ambitions rests on four problems, two of which directly involve non-compliance with the IAEA.

- The first is that Iranian authorities justify their nuclear program as a desire to have indigenous energy security. They can mine uranium inside Iran, enrich it to fuel grade, and then utilize it to operate the eight nuclear reactors they say they wish to build. The problem with this is that they possess only enough indigenous uranium to fuel eight reactors for perhaps 15 years, but for one-third the price, they could upgrade their refinery and pipeline network and fuel their country for more than a century without looking abroad.[1] Clearly, energy security is not their intention.

- The second problem is that while analysts and officials can debate the direction of Iran's current nuclear ambitions, what they cannot dispute is that Iran previously engaged in work which had only military applications—for example, experimenting with nuclear bomb triggers.[2] While the Obama administration pushes its diplomacy on the logic that Iranian President Hassan Rouhani is a reformer, a Deng Xiaoping figure within the Iranian hierarchy, it's important to remember that Iran's bomb work occurred previously under a reformist administration and against the backdrop of the so-called "Dialogue of Civilizations." Either the reformists were insincere, or they simply had no power over Iran's nuclear decision-making. Regardless, the problem starts at the top. White House officials cite Supreme Leader Ali Khamenei's supposed *fatwa* banning nuclear weapons as a sign of his sincerity, but Khamenei's official collection of *fatwas* does not include any such declaration. Meanwhile, numerous Iranian officials have threatened to use nuclear weapons, including several Khamenei appointees and confidantes.[3]

- The third problem is that, unlike with Iraq—where classified intelligence and defector accounts drove intelligence assessments—suspicions with regard to Iran's nuclear program stream from more than a decade of obfuscations and outright lies exposed during IAEA

---

[1] Pacific Northwest Center for Global Security, "Alternative Energy Economics for Iran: Options, Definitions and Evaluation," citing *Uranium 2003 Resources, Production and Demand*, NEA No. 5291, OECD 2004.
[2] David E. Sanger and William J. Broad, "Watchdog Finds Evidence that Iran Worked on Nuclear Triggers," *The New York Times*, May 24, 2011.
[3] For specific instances from Persian sources, see Michael Rubin, "Can Iran be Trusted?" AEI Middle Eastern Outlook, September 2006.

inspections. A careful read of IAEA reports shows a persistent pattern of Iranian officials misleading, obstructing, or outright lying to the IAEA.

- And, the fourth is Iran's refusal to ratify the Additional Protocol. Iran deserves no special rewards for its ratification. By signing the Additional Protocol, it has already received increased access to nuclear technology. By persistently avoiding inspections which kick in after ratification, it suggests its program is not entirely civilian in nature. After all, an above-board, civilian program need not fear inspections, let alone build covert or underground enrichment facilities. At present, Iran only provides the IAEA with carefully managed visits.[4]

It has now been nearly a decade since the International Atomic Energy Agency (IAEA)'s Board of Governors formally found the Islamic Republic of Iran in non-compliance with its Nuclear Non-Proliferation Treaty safe-guards agreement.[5] The reason for the IAEA's finding was, in its words, years of Tehran's "fail[ure] to make important declarations over an extended period of time and in pursuing a policy of concealment up to October 2003;" "continu[ed] gaps in the Agency's understanding of proliferation sensitive aspects of Iran's nuclear programme;" and Iran's "fail[ure]...to re-establish full suspension of all enrichment-related activities." The IAEA also noted that "the Agency is still not in a position to conclude that there are no undeclared nuclear materials or activities in Iran."

Not much has changed. The unfortunate reality is that the same concerns which led to the initial designation of non-compliance remain true today. On March 2, 2015, for example, IAEA head Yukiya Amano implied that Iranian authorities had yet to answer IAEA inquiries. "We have asked questions and the questions are clear, so they can answer," he said.[6] "Iran has yet to provide explanations that enable the agency to clarify two outstanding practical measures," he added.[7] Diplomatic efforts now appear more geared to papering over such non-compliance than resolving it.

There may be more problems to come. In late December 2014, Asghar Zarean, deputy head of the Atomic Energy Organization of Iran, said that Iran would announce advances in laser enrichment on April 9, 2015, Iran's National Nuclear Technology Day in Iran.[8] While Tehran claims that their nuclear laser industry is for medical purposes, the same technology also makes it easier for Iran to secretly build nuclear weapons if the Iranian leadership so chose. Regardless, the development of laser enrichment against the backdrop of ongoing diplomacy contradicts White House claims that Iran has suspended most nuclear work.

The Problem of Possible Military Dimensions

Overlaying Western concerns are the possible military dimensions of the Iranian nuclear program. There is much reason for concern given Iran's pattern of dishonesty and deception. In 2003, the IAEA challenged Tehran to explain the presence of uranium metal in its nuclear fuel cycle, since "neither its

[4] "Implementation of the NPT Safeguards Agreement and relevant provisions of Security Council resolutions in the Islamic Republic of Iran," IAEA Board of Governors, November 7, 2014, GOV/2014/58.
[5] "Implementation of the IAEA Safeguards Agreement in the Islamic Republic of Iran," IAEA Board of Governors, September 24, 2005, GOV/2005/77.
[6] "IAEA head says cannot say when investigation into Iran's nuclear work will end," Reuters, March 2, 2015.
[7] "IAEA says Iran still withholding key information." Reuters, March 2, 2015.
[8] "Iran to Unveil New N. Achievements in April," Fars News (Tehran), January 10, 2015.

light water reactors nor its planned heavy water reactors require uranium metal for fuel."[9] Iran was also in possession of instructions for "casting and machining of enriched and depleted uranium metal into hemispheres."[10] This, of course, could be a central component of a bomb.

The IAEA also has sought clarification on experiments Iran conducted with regard to separation of plutonium during the period when Hassan Rouhani was secretary of the Iran's Supreme National Security Council. The IAEA, however, found inconsistencies between its data and analysis and Iranian explanations.[11] This has become especially important given uncertainties regarding the Arak heavy water reactor which can produce plutonium as a byproduct. Despite the Joint Plan of Action and contrary to Obama administration declarations that Iran has frozen its program, the IAEA continues to find Iran in contravention of IAEA Board of Governors and Security Council resolutions relating to heavy water work.[12]

In 2011, the IAEA provided an annex listing concerns regarding possible military dimensions to Iran's nuclear program.[13] These were numerous, and involved illicit efforts to acquire nuclear material, extraordinary efforts to conceal enrichment from the IAEA, Iran's work on components for an explosive device, Iran's interest in the use of high explosives used to initiate a nuclear detonation, firing systems, modelling work, and integration into a missile delivery vehicle. As of November 2014, the IAEA reported Iran's continued refusal to address its concerns regarding possible military dimensions.[14]

Clearly, it is in the national and international interest to resolve concerns regarding possible military dimensions to Iran's program. Unfortunately, the sunset clause strategy which the Obama administration is now pursuing in negotiations may make this impossible. In order to verify the completeness of South Africa's declaration of inventory of nuclear material and facilities, the IAEA went back more than two decades into South Africa's nuclear program.[15] The Islamic Republic of Iran refuses to provide a similar baseline, making IAEA verification impossible. Indeed, it appears the White House is sacrificing the IAEA's ability to do its job in order to win an unverifiable and incomplete deal.

Was North Korea a "Teachable Moment?"

There is an unfortunate pattern I detail in my recent book, *Dancing with the Devil: The Perils of Engaging Rogue Regimes*: Once high-level diplomatic processes start, the White House and State Department are loathe to see them end. Second term presidencies only exacerbate the problem as political

---

[9] "Implementation of the NPR safeguards agreement in the Islamic Republic of Iran," IAEA Board of Governors, June 6, 2003, GOV/2003/40.

[10] "Implementation of the NPR safeguards agreement in the Islamic Republic of Iran," IAEA Board of Governors, June 6, 2003, GOV/2003/40.

[11] "Implementation of the NPR safeguards agreement in the Islamic Republic of Iran," IAEA Board of Governors, April 28, 2006, GOV/2006/27.

[12] "Implementation of the NPT Safeguards Agreement and relevant provisions of Security Council resolutions in the Islamic Republic of Iran," IAEA Board of Governors, November 7, 2014, GOV/2014/58.

[13] "Implementation of the NPT Safeguards Agreement and relevant provisions of Security Council resolutions in the Islamic Republic of Iran," IAEA Board of Governors, November 8, 2011, GOV/2011/65.

[14] "Implementation of the NPT Safeguards Agreement and relevant provisions of Security Council resolutions in the Islamic Republic of Iran," IAEA Board of Governors, November 7, 2014, GOV/2014/58.

[15] Adolf von Baeckmann, Garry Dillon, and Demetrius Perricos, "Nuclear Verification in South Africa," *IAEA Bulletin*, January 1995.

considerations and quest for legacy sometimes trump prudence. The security concerns which sparked the initial diplomacy become subordinate to the desire to keep opponents at the table. Signing a deal becomes more important than the substance of that deal.

A case in point is the Agreed Framework with North Korea which this past October marked its 20th anniversary. Barely a month into the Clinton presidency, the North Korean regime stopped IAEA inspections and soon after announced its impending withdraw from the Nuclear Non-Proliferation Treaty. Unwilling to take any path that could lead to military action, Clinton's team sought to talk Pyongyang down from its nuclear defiance. Clinton's very willingness to negotiate North Korea's nuclear compliance was a concession, however, since the 1953 armistice agreement demanded that Pyongyang reveal all military facilities and, in case of dispute, enable the Military Armistice Commission to determine the purpose of suspect facilities. By making weaker nonproliferation frameworks the new baseline, Clinton let North Korea off the hook before talks even began. It's a model that Obama repeated with Iran. After all, six unanimous or nearly unanimous UN Security Council Resolutions demanded a complete cessation of Iranian enrichment, a requirement which Obama waived to get Iran to the table.

Just as it does today with Iran, however, the IAEA held firmer to the demands for North Korean compliance than did American negotiators who feared too strict a verification and inspection regimen might undercut the possibility of a deal. The issue came to a head in September 1993 after the State Department pressured the IAEA to compromise on limited inspections. The IAEA let alone the United Nations Security Council have been clear with respect to Iran's obligations, but the Obama administration has allowed Iran a path to noncompliance for the sake of keeping diplomacy alive. Not surprisingly, given an inch, Tehran took a mile.

The North Korea example remains relevant today for two other reasons:

- First, even if the idea behind the North Korea formula had been solid, in hindsight it is clear that the Agreed Framework failed to prevent North Korea's nuclear breakout.

- Second, the Iranian leadership looks at North Korea's nuclear program as a model to emulate rather than an example to condemn. In 2005, the Iranian nuclear negotiator Hossein Mousavian, who remains a persistent voice of praise for the current process, bragged about the earlier round of talks under President Mohammad Khatami, "During these two years of negotiations, we managed to make far greater progress than North Korea."[16] Iranian negotiators still win by the same standard. The sunset clause offered by the Obama administration to remove enrichment limitations on Iran after a decade afford the Islamic Republic a path to the bomb two years quicker than North Korea achieved.

Is a Bad Deal Better Than No Deal?
There is no doubt that the United States can reach a deal with the Islamic Republic of Iran if the Obama administration continues to abandon its own redlines but adhere to respect Supreme Leader Ali Khamenei's. Rewarding intransigence never brings compromise; it only encourages continued Iranian non-compliance with its obligations to the IAEA. Nor, after years of cheating, does limiting inspections to the IAEA regimen make sense: The IAEA is only able by its own bylaws to inspect

---

[16] Victor Davis Hanson, "Should we fix Gaza, Iran and N. Korea?" *Chicago Tribune*, August 19, 2005.

declared nuclear sites. This is why the IAEA Board of Governors have been quite precise only saying that Iran has not enriched uranium hexafluoride above 5 percent in any of its declared facilities since the Joint Plan of Action took effect.[17] The Islamic Republic has a long history of maintain clandestine sites spanning from Natanz to Fordo and now, according to recent revelations, to Lavizan-3. Even if the international community saw truckloads of highly enriched uranium or plutonium entering or exiting an undeclared site, the IAEA would not be able to inspect it should Iran refuse to declare it as a nuclear facility.

Shortly before stepping down as secretary of Iran's Supreme National Security Council, Hassan Rouhani gave a speech at Ferdowsi University in Mashhad, in which he reviewed his strategy as Iran's nuclear negotiator as well as U.S.-Iran relations. "What we were able to do was to make the opposite of whatever America predicted occur," he declared. He crowed triumphant: "What the Islamic Republic of Iran has done in this period has been a great and complex task. Iran was alone and no one supported it. Despite all this we were able to show this power of maneuvering to the world and with divine grace and power we will continue the rest of the way…" Lest anyone question what he meant, he explained, "The basis of the discussion is that a nation that has the power to prepare nuclear power plant fuel also has the power to produce an atomic bomb."[18] Who could have ever expected that over the course of an 18-month diplomatic process, more than a decade of Iranian non-compliance with the IAEA would be waived, and Tehran would be handed the path to, in Rouhani's words, "the power to produce an atomic bomb."

---

[17] "Implementation of the NPT Safeguards Agreement and relevant provisions of Security Council resolutions in the Islamic Republic of Iran," IAEA Board of Governors, November 7, 2014, GOV/2014/58.

[18] Hassan Rouhani, "Iran's Measures Rob the Americans of Foresight," as published in *Rahbord* (Tehran) [the journal of the Expediency Council's Center for Strategic Studies], Spring 2005.

Statement for the Record
Submitted by Mr. Connolly of Virginia

Verification, transparency, and compliance will be paramount to the viability of any comprehensive nuclear agreement with Iran. Iran's past transgressions have led to a profound lack of trust of Tehran by the U.S. and the international community, and we remain in a formative period of engagement. It will be incumbent upon Iran to build a substantial record of compliance before the U.S. and our P5+1 partners are confident that the Iran nuclear program is exclusively peaceful in nature.

According to the International Atomic Energy Agency (IAEA), Iran has started down a path of compliance under the Joint Plan of Action (JPOA). The JPOA has demonstrated that an effective nuclear agreement can constrain Iran's nuclear program. The JPOA has arrested the Iran nuclear program on several fronts and has actually reversed gains Iran made while developing its program outside the purview of international inspectors. Before the JPOA went into effect, Iran was enriching uranium stockpiles, constructing a heavy water reactor at Arak, readying 9,000 additional centrifuges for operation, and allowing inspectors only sporadic access to nuclear facilities. Under the JPOA, Iran has eliminated all 20 percent enriched uranium, suspended all enrichment above 5 percent, stopped construction at Arak, kept 9,000 centrifuges offline, and provided inspectors with daily access to its nuclear facilities.

However, this relatively brief record of adherence does not negate the fact that Iran has previously flaunted the IAEA safeguards agreement resulting in several rebukes from the international community. The UN Security Council has passed six resolutions addressing Iran's nuclear program since 2006, four of which placed punitive restrictions on Tehran. As recently as February 2015, the IAEA Board of Governors certified Iran's lack of engagement regarding the potential military dimensions of its nuclear program. I joined a bipartisan coalition of 367 Members of Congress in writing to President Obama to state that a full understanding of the potential military dimensions of Iran's nuclear program would be integral to a final nuclear agreement.

It should be noted that Iran has not operated under the IAEA Additional Protocol since 2006. The Additional Protocol is a legal document that allows the IAEA to verify both declared and undeclared nuclear material and activities. A high-quality nuclear agreement would almost certainly include a verification regime that affords inspectors the freedom of initiative provided under the Additional Protocol. Under previously successful verification provisions in South Africa, the IAEA sought assurances that all nuclear material had been placed under IAEA safeguards and was for solely peaceful purposes, all nuclear equipment had been destroyed, all nuclear weapons-related facilities ceased weapons-related operations, and that any new nuclear weapons activity could be detected going forward. Commensurate and independently verified assurances from Iran will be fundamental to any nuclear agreement.

Blocking Iran's pathways to the bomb through a nuclear agreement is our best available option for preventing Iran from obtaining a nuclear weapon. However, an agreement will not be defined by accommodation from the international community. It will instead be Iran's responsibility to bring its nuclear program in full view of international inspectors and strictly adhere to the terms an agreement. It is the policy of the United States that Iran will not obtain a nuclear weapon, and that black and white policy will not tolerate ambiguity in an agreement's verification regime.